WINNING WELL

WINNING WELL

A MANAGER'S GUIDE
TO GETTING RESULTS—
WITHOUT LOSING YOUR SOUL

Karin Hurt and David Dye

Foreword by Marshall Goldsmith,
author of *Triggers* and *Mojo*

AMACOM
American Management Association
New York • Atlanta • Brussels • Chicago • Mexico City • San Francisco
Shanghai • Tokyo • Toronto • Washington, D.C.

Bulk discounts available. For details visit:
www.amacombooks.org/go/specialsales
Or contact special sales:
Phone: 800-250-5308
Email: specialsls@amanet.org
View all the AMACOM titles at: www.amacombooks.org
American Management Association: www.amanet.org

This publication is designed to provide accurate and authoritative information in regard to the subject matter covered. It is sold with the understanding that the publisher is not engaged in rendering legal, accounting, or other professional service. If legal advice or other expert assistance is required, the services of a competent professional person should be sought.

Net Promoter Score is a registered trademark of Fred Reichheld, Bain & Company
Diaper Genie is a registered trademark of Playtex Products, Inc.

LIBRARY OF CONGRESS CATALOGING-IN-PUBLICATION DATA
Names: Hurt, Karin, Dye, David, authors.
Title: Winning well: a manager's guide to getting results—without losing your
    soul/Karin Hurt and David Dye; foreword by Marshall Goldsmith.
Description: New York: American Management Association, [2016] | Includes
    index.
Identifiers: LCCN 2015045507 (print) | LCCN 2015047288 (ebook) | ISBN
    9780814437254 (hardcover) | ISBN 9780814437261 (ebook)
Subjects: LCSH: Executive ability. | Management. | Performance. | Leadership.
Classificiation: LCC HD38.2.H87 2016 (print) | LCC HD38.2 (ebook) | DDC
    658.4/09—dc23
LC record available at http://lccn.loc.gov/2015045507

About AMA
American Management Association (www.amanet.org) is a world leader in talent development, advancing the skills of individuals to drive business success. Our mission is to support the goals of individuals and organizations through a complete range of products and services, including classroom and virtual seminars, webcasts, webinars, podcasts, conferences, corporate and government solutions, business books, and research. AMA's approach to improving performance combines experiential learning—learning through doing—with opportunities for ongoing professional growth at every step of one's career journey.

To my parents, Larry and Jean,
my first and best examples of winning well.
And to Marcus, Ben and Sebastian
on our shared journey toward what's possible.
—Karin

To my daughter, Averie,
for showing me what it means to win well.
—David

Contents

SECTION 3

Winning Well—Motivate, Inspire, and Energize Your Team

SECTION 4

It's Time to Win Well

Foreword

I've made a career out of helping business leaders develop better relationships with their colleagues and team. In the course of that work, I've seen many managers who struggle to achieve business success, much less build meaningful professional relationships.

If that's you, you're not alone. The truth is that in companies, nonprofits, and government offices around the world, it's not hard to find stressed-out, frustrated (and often helpless) managers. But it doesn't have to be this way. Not for you.

Karin Hurt and David Dye give you the tools you need to take on a manager's most important job: to improve business performance, without sacrificing your humanity, your well-being, or your sanity.

I often share with executives that the only performance appraisal that really matters is the one you give yourself as you look back over your life. When friends of mine interviewed people in the last years of their life, three themes emerged: be happy now, friends and family are critically important, and if you have a dream, go for it.

From a business perspective, my ultimate business advice isn't very different:

- Life is short—have fun.

- Do whatever you can to help people.

- Do what you think is right.

Karin and David give you the specific tools to accomplish all three of these goals in your daily work. The resources they share will help you create a healthy management mindset, improve business performance with less stress, and help you build better relation-ships with your colleagues and team. I encourage you to use these tools, not just because they will improve your business performance but also because at the end of your life, you will be happy that you did.

As an executive coach, I'm fond of simple tools. Yet simple doesn't mean easy. The tools Karin and David share with you are straightforward and simple to implement, but they will work only when you use them. Karin and David know they work because they've been where you are now, and they've practiced everything they give you.

One thing that sets Karin and David apart from other business authors is their compassion. They genuinely know what it's like to do the work you do, face the pressures you do, and thrive amid them. They have genuine compassion for frontline and middle-level man-agers that comes through in the encouragement, humor, and tough love they share. They want you to succeed.

Ultimately, your work as a manager is about far more than what you make or how you serve your customers. In the final chapter, Karin and David call us to our legacy: the life you build for yourself, your family, and the impact you have on the people around you while you do your work. In *Winning Well,* Karin and David give you the answers you need to do just that. Will you use them?

Life is good.

MARSHALL GOLDSMITH,
AUTHOR OF *TRIGGERS* **AND** *MOJO*

WINNING WELL

WINNING
WELL

The World of Winning Well

Welcome to a new way to manage: the world of Winning Well. Throughout this book we give you the tools to thrive, achieve lasting business results, and enjoy your work. In this section we introduce the very real challenges that confront every manager, explain what exactly we mean by Winning Well, and give you the fundamental principles you can use to succeed in every management scenario you encounter. You'll also meet three types of managers who either aren't winning or are winning poorly and losing their soul in the process. Finally, we'll share how to manage effectively in the age of constant data. These tools are your foundation to win well and get results without losing your soul.

CHAPTER 1

Winning Well

"Life is either a daring adventure or nothing at all."
—HELEN KELLER

Too often, managers try to win at all costs, when they should be focused on Winning Well. The hypercompetitive postrecession global economy puts frontline and middle-level managers in a difficult position—expected to win, to "move the needle," to get the highest ratings, rankings, and results. Many managers become hell-bent on winning no matter what it takes, and they treat people like objects—in short, they lose their soul.

This exacts a high price from managers as they work longer hours to try to keep up. Those unwilling to make this trade-off either leave for a less-competitive environment or try to stave off the performance demands by "being nice" to their team. After years of trying to win while sandwiched between the employees who do the heavy lifting and leaders above them piling on more, they give up and try to get along. Inevitably, after prolonged stress and declining performance, they surrender to apathy, disengage, or get fired.

Don't think this is happening where you work? Research says otherwise. According to Gallup, nearly two-thirds of American workers and managers are disengaged.[1] We don't believe that's a coincidence. No one wins in environments like that.

• • •

"You can't be in last place!" Joe shouted, and immediately winced as he saw Ann's exhausted eyes begin to tear up.

Later in his office, Joe admitted: "She didn't deserve that. She's a newly promoted center director working long hours in a fast ramp-up. The problem is, we're out of time. The business plan called for this center to be profitable in six months, and it's been over a year, and we're not even close. My VP keeps calling for updates every few hours, and that just wastes everyone's time."

Joe squeezed his temples. "My people need me to coach and support them, but if we don't improve in the next 90 days, none of us will be here next year. Maybe I need to go."

Joe leads a 600-person call center. The company stack ranks employees, meaning that every representative is assessed on a balanced scorecard of quality, productivity, and financials and ranked in order from highest to lowest. The managers and centers are ranked in the same way, and Joe's center is dead last. The vice president of operations keeps a close eye on those numbers and constantly calls Joe to ask what he's doing about the ranking. Joe spends most of his time putting out fires, answering customer complaints, and crunching numbers in a desperate attempt to move his team up the stack rank.

Whether your organization stack ranks or not, can you identify with Joe's frustration? He's been asked to win a game that feels rigged. He can't possibly do everything he needs to. The company keeps score, and Joe is losing. Every time he tries to win, he ends up hurting people—people he knows are trying as hard as he is.

At this point, he's not sure he can win, but if he can, it seems that victory will cost him dearly. He can feel his soul slipping away every time he loses his temper. It gets results—but at what cost?

WINNING

Winning doesn't mean you reach some imaginary state of perfection. Winning means that you and your people succeed at doing what you're there to do. The real competition isn't the department across the building or the organization across town. Your competition is mediocrity.

Whether you manage a group of engineers with a government contract to build the next interplanetary satellite, or you supervise a nonprofit team working to save an endangered shrew, or you manage a team of property tax assessors in a large city, or you're a surgeon working with an anesthesiologist and operating room nurses you've never met before to save a patient's life, or you manage a 24-hour convenience store, winning means you achieve excellence. When you win, we have better customer service, better products, better care, better experiences, and a better world. When you win, life is better for everyone.

WINNING WELL

Winning Well means that you sustain excellent performance over time, because you refuse to succumb to harsh, stress-inducing shortcuts that temporarily scare people into "performing." You need energized, motivated people all working together. Your strategy is only as strong as the ability of your people to execute at the front line, and if they're too scared or tired to think, they won't. You can have all the great plans, six sigma quality programs, and brilliant competitive positioning in the universe, but if the human beings doing the real work lack the competence, confidence, and creativity to pull it off, you're finished.

In fact, in today's connected world, people increasingly expect a positive work environment. When you don't provide it, they can easily go across the street to your competitor or go into business for themselves as freelancers or independent contractors. Now everyone else but you benefits from the time and training you invested.

Winning Well means that you sustain excellent performance over time.

The stories and best practices in this book come from our experience working with thousands of managers across private, public, and nonprofit industries who have something in common: They must motivate their people to achieve results that often feel impossible. Winning Well doesn't mean you'll be a pushover. It means you'll be a manager known for getting results, whom people respect, and whom people want to work with. You can win—and you can win without losing your soul.

HOW TO USE THIS BOOK

In *Winning Well*, we share proven, practical tools you can use to inspire your people and achieve excellent results over time. These are the same tools we used in our own careers and we share with all the managers we train and coach. This isn't a book about management theory; we give you enough context so you can understand why something works and how to adapt it for your needs, but our goal is to give you resources you can use right away not just to win—but to win well.

Winning Well is written so you can quickly find the answers you need. We recommend that you read it through and answer the action plan questions at the end of each chapter. You can also use the book as a real-world reference guide for challenges you face. Have a team member who feels left out or needs more challenge? Turn to Chapter 17 or Chapter 19 and solve your problem. Do delegated tasks slip through your fingers? Check out Chapter 9. If you're looking for a quick activity to energize your team or build better relationships, flip through Section 3 and you'll find several that meet your needs.

Every chapter includes real-life examples taken from our experiences or those of the many managers we've worked with. At the conclusion of every chapter is Your Winning Well Action Plan. The questions and activities in these sections are designed to help you apply what you've learned and see changes as soon as possible. Each section ends with a summary of the Winning Well practices essential to your success.

In the next chapter, we'll share the management mindset that is the core of Winning Well. You can take this model with you into any scenario you'll ever encounter and win well. Section 1 concludes with recommendations on how to use data without letting it distract you from what's ultimately important.

In Section 2, Chapters 4 to 11, we give you tools that allow you to win—to achieve meaningful results. These are practical tips, techniques, and tactics you can apply immediately to address performance-related issues, including how to get your people focused on results, how to make business decisions everyone gets behind, and how to quickly hold your people accountable for commitments and results.

In the third section of the book, Chapters 12 to 21 provide you the keys to win well—to motivate, inspire, and energize your team. You will dive into the fundamental needs all employee have and explore practical methods for supporting them in ways that sustain and improve results.

In the final section, Chapters 22 to 25 address challenges you'll encounter on your Winning Well journey. Section 4 gives you specific ways to overcome bosses who don't care if you win well, employees who don't care if they win at all, and perhaps the most difficult challenge—you.

YOUR WINNING WELL ACTION PLAN

In addition to the tools in the book, we've included a wealth of additional resources, appendixes, activities, and handouts in the Winning Well Tool Kit available online at www.WinningWellBook.com. We recommend you download the tool kit and keep it nearby as you read.

NOTES

1. Nikki Blacksmith and Jim Harter, "Majority of American Workers Not Engaged in Their Jobs," Gallup Poll, October 28, 2011, accessed October 15, 2014, http://www.gallup.com/poll/150383/Majority-American-Workers-Not-Engaged-Jobs.aspx; "State of the American Manager: Analytics and Advice for Leaders," Gallup report, October 28, 2011, accessed January 11, 2015, http://www.gallup.com/services/182138/state-american-manager.aspx.

2. Intuit's research predicts that by 2020, 40 percent of the American workforce will be freelancers. Intuit, "Intuit 2020 Report," October 2010, accessed April 3, 2015, http://http-download.intuit.com/http.intuit/CMO/intuit/futureofsmallbusiness/intuit_2020_report.pdf.

CHAPTER 2

How to Win Well in Every Situation

---

*"'Think simple' as my old master used to say—
meaning reduce the whole of its parts into the
simplest terms, getting back to first principles."*
—FRANK LLOYD WRIGHT

I n this chapter we share four foundational Winning Well principles: confidence, humility, results, and relationships. In the
Action Plan at the end of this chapter you can complete a Winning
Well assessment to identify areas where you already excel, and
behaviors that could use additional focus.

• • •

"Don't throw fish!"

There aren't many places you'd hear that sentence spoken—
unless you spend time in children's classrooms. Then, all bets are
off.

David began his professional career as an educator. When you're
trained as a teacher, one of the most important professional skills
you ever learn is how to manage your classroom. How do you create
and maintain a safe learning environment and keep 30 (or more)

students focused when many of them would rather be doing something else? How do you prevent misbehavior?

Early in his teaching career, a mentor shared an important principle of classroom management. She called it the "Don't throw fish" paradigm. When it comes to classroom management, inexperienced teachers often default to a list of rules. You'll remember these from your own classroom days: raise your hand to speak, keep your hands to yourself, and stay in line.

But what do you do when a student does something that isn't covered by the rules? Say, for example, he throws a ball at a classmate. The inexperienced teacher says, "Don't throw balls at people."

That's when little Tommy, who ought to be a lawyer when he grows up, grabs a goldfish out of the classroom aquarium and throws it at Susie. The exasperated teacher yells, "Tommy, didn't I tell you not to throw things at people?"

Tommy, impish grin firmly in place, says, "You said don't throw balls—you didn't say anything about fish."

The point David's mentor made is this: You'll never have a specific rule for everything. It is far more useful to have a few simple, straightforward guidelines that apply all the time.

We share many specific tools you can use in specific situations and to achieve specific results, but we don't address every situation you'll ever experience. We can do better. We can give you the Winning Well principles—the model and practices that will get you through any management or leadership situation you'll ever face. When you master these, you'll be ready for anything. In fact, all of the specific tools we give throughout the rest of the book are built on these principles.

THE FOUR PRINCIPLES OF WINNING WELL

Managers who sustain results over time operate from four principles. Internally, they value confidence and humility. Externally, they build on this strong internal foundation with a combined focus on relationships and results. Let's start with confidence, because yours will inspire others' and make the other three principles easier to enact. There are three critical components to managing with confidence: know your strengths, stand up for what matters, and speak the truth.

CONFIDENCE

1. Know your strengths, own them, and use them.

You don't need to manage exactly like anyone else, but you do need to be confident in who you are and what you bring to the table. If you don't believe in yourself, your employees won't either.

One time Karin went on a western cattle roundup with her family. Their young cowgirl guide, Jo, was calm under pressure, clearly knew what she was doing, and kept all the city folk safe. If one of the riders lost control and found himself and his horse surrounded by cows, she'd shout out, "You're a cow," as a fun but clear reminder to get the person back to safety.

Unfortunately for Jo, she lacked confidence. Apart from the high-pressure moments, she undercut her own strengths by saying things like, "Oh, I am not very good at getting people's attention. I really talk too much; it's not good; sometimes I just can't stop talking. I'm sure you would have had a better experience if my brother had led the ride."

Karin watched as people were leaving and saw how Jo's lack of confidence reduced her tips. She had taught the city slickers how much to value her.

Just like Jo's words, your words will teach your employees what to think of you. It didn't matter that she was a young woman. Imagine if Jo had said, "I've been herding cattle with my daddy from the time I was in diapers. Follow me and you'll learn some fun techniques and we'll have a successful evening. Ignore me, and . . . well, that can be dangerous. Now saddle up!"

You have strengths. The more you know what they are, own them, and use them, the more your people can respect you.

2. Stand up for what matters.

Jo let a lot of stuff go at the beginning of the session that turned out to be disruptive and annoying. One well-to-do family was quite disorganized and ignored her 17 calls to get their act together. All the other participants ended up waiting for them, which cut into the time for their cattle drive.

A more confident start would have gone a long way. Imagine if Jo had said, "Safety first on this mission. Everyone needs closed-toed shoes, a helmet, and some water. We leave precisely at 5:00 p.m., otherwise the bulls are likely to get a little crazy. If you're not here at five, we'll have to leave without you. Any questions?"

3. Speak the truth.

Your influence and credibility naturally improve when you speak the truth. Confidence is your belief in yourself and your ability to handle what comes your way. When you fail to speak the truth, you undercut your ability to trust yourself.

The most difficult and most important part of speaking the truth is being willing to share tough feedback and deliver bad news— up, down, and sideways. Winning Well means being willing to tell your boss the project is in jeopardy, to tell your peer that his negative attitude is impacting morale, to tell your direct report her body odor could get in the way of her career aspirations, or to admit to yourself that the way you've been doing things isn't working and it's time to learn a new skill.

• • •

Confidence is a critical internal value, but it becomes more powerful when paired with humility. Humility does not mean putting yourself down or allowing other people to treat you poorly. As an internal management value, humility means that you have an accurate self-image. You know your strengths and you know your challenges. You recognize your internal worth and you also recognize and respect the dignity and worth of every human being.

HUMILITY

1. Have an accurate self-image.

Early in her career, Karin was leading a human resources (HR) team sent in to "recover" a troubled call center in the Bronx, New York. Absenteeism was at 22 percent. Results were horrible. The center was in danger of closing, and the reps were in danger of losing jobs they really needed.

The team brought in trainers, found day care, did recognition, and used every other employee engagement trick you can imagine. Sure enough, they cut absenteeism in half, results improved, and the manager was promoted. They declared victory and went back to their regular jobs.

As Karin walked out the door, Juanita, a slender team leader with oversized clothes and a big heart, hugged her and said, "Thank you. We couldn't have done it without you."

At the time, Karin took that as a compliment. However, she later came to regret the irony in Juanita's generous words.

Two months later, results had returned to exactly where they had started, only now, leadership morale was worse.

This is when Karin learned her most important leadership lesson: The true sign of leadership is what happens when the leader walks away. "We couldn't have done it without you" was a flashing neon sign. This was not a sign that Karin had done well; it was a sign that she had screwed up. The people did not believe they could do it themselves, and within two months of her leaving, their behavior followed their beliefs because the success had come from an external solution.

Good leadership is never about what you can do, it's about what you enable and encourage others to achieve.

2. Admit mistakes.

When she realized the irony in Juanita's gratitude, Karin called the vice president who had sent her to the Bronx, admitted her mistake, and asked for a second chance.

Then she flew back to the call center and tried again, this time from behind the scenes—ensuring that Juanita and the other team leaders called the shots, managed the project, and implemented the plan. Results improved, a bit more gradually, but this time they lasted.

Nothing inspires a team more than admitting you've made a mistake, but first you've got to admit it to yourself—a vital starting point for humility.

3. Invite challengers.

Have you ever known an employee who was a Mini-Me of his boss? They dress the same, have the same personal interests, laugh at the same jokes, and even have some of the same habits. The boss loves this guy because he can even finish sentences for him; after all, "great minds think alike." The employee loves it because it feels so good to be someone's favorite and, let's face it, riding someone's coattails is often a way to get promoted quickly.

This Mini-Me grooming may appear to work for a while, but sooner or later the failure to consider alternative perspectives will lead to poor decisions. Plus, both people are likely to lose credibility as they begin to be viewed as a package deal, unable to have an independent thought. It takes humility to surround yourself with people who will challenge your thinking. (In Chapter 16, we give you specific tools do this well.)

• • •

Focusing on results exclusively may improve outcomes for a time while also burning out employees, increasing apathy, and killing morale. We've seen too many managers end up isolated, frustrated, and working harder just to keep results from getting worse because they're caught in this vicious circle. With just a little more focus on relationships, though, you can inspire people to commit more deeply to their goals.

You might also know managers who focus exclusively on relationships, creating caring and supportive environments but with little to no accountability for results. The A-players inevitably flee because the best talent wants to work on a winning team, and if you don't care enough to build one, they'll find one somewhere else.

Once again, you don't have to choose between results and relationships. Effective managers focus on both. We'll discuss results first. After all, achieving results is what the "Winning" in Winning Well is all about. There are three keys to staying focused on results: clarify, plan, and do.

RESULTS

1. Clarify.

One of the most important responsibilities you have as a Winning Well manager is to ensure clarity. Your people need to understand why your group exists, what results you are accountable to produce, the impact of your work, and what success looks like. When we work with an organization, we tell the managers that we can test this very easily. We should be able to ask any employee, "What does your work group do, and why do those results matter to the organization?" Within a team or work group the answers should be the same.

Clarity starts with an internal process. Before you can articulate your vision with clarity, you've got to be sure you really know yourself. This means taking the company vision and investing some time thinking about what your group does and why it matters.

Christie was a nursing manager in a high-pressure public hospital. She was energetic, persuasive, and popular. Ultimately, however, she was replaced. Even though her supervisors liked her, her nurses thought well of her, and she was fun to work with, she didn't provide clarity about the results her department needed to achieve. She lost her job because she didn't clearly state what winning looked like nor establish tangible goals and objectives that ensured a patient-centered, error-free environment.

2. Plan.

With the purpose and results clear to everyone, managers who win well work hard to create tight plans that will make these results happen. You do this through clear, outcome-focused decision making that helps your people imagine more than they would otherwise, with intentional meetings, delegation that get things done, and efficient problem solving. Keep everyone focused on the outcomes and the steps it will take to get there, and you build clear commitments to one another.

Christie resisted creating plans. She enjoyed the relational aspects of her work with other nurses and interactions with the patients. However, without even basic checklists, essential activities such as briefing patients on their home care were lacking. The infrequent meetings she was able to hold turned into gripe fests that broke into multiple side conversations, and no one was clear on what they were supposed to do differently following the meeting.

3. Do.

Achieving results starts with clarity and intentional plans, and it concludes with what you and your people actually do. Without intentional action there are no results. Winning Well managers are masters of action and accountability. You and your people do what you said you would do, you hold one another accountable for your commitments, celebrate success, and review what you've done to learn what went well and what you want to do differently next time.

Without clarity of outcomes, a clear plan to get there, and mutual commitments to action, Christie's team floundered. They did the best they could to care for their patients in the moment, but they were consistently overwhelmed, running around to take care of loose ends with doctors' orders, paperwork, and home-care instructions that could have been avoided. Finally, they were frustrated that nurses who didn't perform were not held accountable.

A clear and effective focus on results is the foundation for your influence and success as a manager. You cannot win without it.

• • •

Winning means you achieve results, but those results don't become sustainable until you add the second external focus of relationships. This focus on relationships includes three key activities: connect, invest, and collaborate.

RELATIONSHIPS

1. Connect.

Management focus on relationships doesn't mean you try to be best friends with all of your employees. It does mean you connect with your people as human beings. You treat everyone with respect and dignity, not as a number, object, or problem. You build trust with, and between, your people; you listen to their values, needs, and insights; and you encourage their success.

Rich was a product manager for a national software company. His product team enjoyed hanging out with him after work. Over a beer or a sandwich, Rich was a kind, approachable person. At work, however, he changed. He got things done, but it came at a high price. He disconnected from his employees as human beings, and nothing his team produced was ever good enough. He drove his people to work six or seven days every week without a break. Rich's mantra was, "We've got to produce." After he replaced his team several times, the company finally encouraged Rich to take early retirement following a stress-induced heart attack. Rich lacked a healthy connection—with his people and with himself.

2. Invest.

You recognize and value that each of your employees has unique strengths and perspectives. You draw out the strengths, talents, and skills from people while helping them minimize their liabilities. Your employees know you care about them as people as you help them grow, becoming more effective and productive.

Investing takes time to look at a person's potential to perform beyond her current role, to challenge her to take on tasks she may feel are beyond her, and to scaffold her as she builds confidence.

Bryan is one of the best managers we've ever seen in action. An executive-level manager in a global accounting firm, he was legendary within his division for seeing the strength and potential in people. One employee, Grace, shared how Bryan approached her when she was, in her words, "just a secretary." He told her she was good at her job and he'd seen how she took other administrative assistants under her wing to help them learn how to do the job. Then he asked her if she'd like to learn how to train executive assistants around the world. "Imagine that," she said. "I was from a small town in Arkansas, and I ended up traveling around the world doing work I loved because Bryan saw me."

Where other managers might have been irritated by the time Grace took to work with the new assistants, Bryan saw potential and invested in it.

3. Collaborate.

Collaboration is more than simply working together. It's an attitude that communicates you are in it with your people, not apart from them.

Early in David's career, a coworker, Juan, approached him with a hard truth: "In that last conversation with our supervisor, she asked about us, but you kept saying, 'I did this . . . I'm doing that.' I know you're the team leader, but I wonder if you realize I'm here. How about some 'we' next time?" Juan helped David learn that while you may have different responsibilities, your people are working with you, not for you.

• • •

Confidence, humility, results, and relationships are the essential characteristics of managers who win well. The challenge for most of us is that we naturally gravitate toward one or two of these elements more than the others. The most effective managers, however, don't stop there. They combine confidence and humility; they focus on results and relationships. Let's examine how these characteristics interact (see Figure 2.1).

FOUR TYPES OF MANAGERS

Each of these internal values and external focuses interact to create one of four manager types. To better understand the principles of managers who win well, take a look at each of the four manager types.

The User

In the upper left quadrant are managers who work to win at any cost. We call them Users because they tend to see people as objects to be used in order to get results.

FIGURE 2.1. THE FOUR MANAGER TYPES.

USER MANAGER	WINNING WELL MANAGER
Values: Confidence > Humility Results > Relationships	**Values:** Confidence and humility Results and relationships
Focus: Short-term results	**Focus:** Focus on both long and short time horizons
Behaviors: More energy for less results Longer hours Abusive	**Behaviors:** High expectations Healthy professional relationships Activity and accountability
Outcomes: Stress Unsustainable turnover Bitter Frustrated Feels like a victim	**Outcomes:** Sustainable results over time *Fulfilled:* enjoys work and life Low turnover *Respected:* people want to work with Sense of efficacy and influence
GAMER MANAGER	PLEASER MANAGER
Values: Self-preservation Status	**Values:** Humility > Confidence Relationships > Results
Focus: Short-term survival and status	**Focus:** Day-to-day focus on being liked
Behaviors: Manipulation "Dirty" politics Divide and conquer Plays games to hang on, outlast	**Behaviors:** Politics of hiding Reactive Little accountability
Outcomes: Attracts unhealthy employees Productive employees leave	**Outcomes:** Stress Top performers leave Feels like a victim No results

VALUES:

User managers value confidence above humility. They prioritize results above relationships.

FOCUS:

User managers focus on short-term results. They emphasize getting things done today and will worry about tomorrow when it gets here.

BEHAVIORS:

User managers tend to treat people as objects—the people are there to achieve results and that is their only value. These managers push hard for results and try to compel productivity through fear, power, and control. At the extreme they say things like, "If you don't like it, leave" and, "Why should I say thank you? It's their job." They do not offer relevant encouragement and are inconsistent with accountability, often becoming reactionary and explosive when frustrated with poor results. Their meetings are often one-way information dumps with requests for input met with silence. Meetings also end in silence, which the manager mistakes for agreement.

OUTCOMES:

People—User managers create work environments that resemble sweatshops. They do achieve results, but at a high cost. Their employees do the least possible to avoid punishment. People leave as soon as they can afford to. Employees don't solve problems or take initiative; they are happy to leave those tasks to their manager.

Manager—Since they get things done through fear, power, and control they have to spend a tremendous amount of energy policing their workers, forcing people to work, and replacing employees who leave. They often feel out of control (since they can't possibly control everything or everyone). Frequently, these managers are frustrated, bitter, stressed, and suffer from poor physical and emotional health.

The Pleaser

In the lower right quadrant are managers who aren't trying to win but do put effort into amiable relationships with their colleagues. We call them Pleasers because they spend most of their energy trying to be liked by other people.

VALUES:

Pleaser managers value humility above confidence, and the confidence they do have derives from how well they perceive they are liked by others. They prioritize relationships above results.

FOCUS:

Pleaser managers have a short time horizon. They work hard to ensure that people think well of them today.

BEHAVIORS:

Their short-term focus on being liked drives Pleasers to reactionary behaviors depending on who doesn't like them today. These swings in behavior can make Pleasers seem wildly unpredictable. When an employee comes to a Pleaser with a problem, the Pleaser will often try to fix it. Paradoxically, in the attempt to be liked by one person, a Pleaser can verbally abuse or publicly humiliate another person without realizing it. When the humiliated employee confronts the Pleaser manager, the Pleaser will often apologize and say something like, "I don't know what to do" or, "I just want everyone to be happy."

Pleasers rarely practice accountability unless someone pushes them to do so. When they do, their accountability is often insincere and ineffective since they are really just trying to make another person happy. Until their poor results catch up with them, Pleaser work groups and meetings can feel like happy hour—lots of fun and feel good, but no appreciable progress or commitments. They put a significant amount of time into the politics of hiding. They schmooze other managers and supervisors trying to maintain good will and avoid accountability for poor results.

OUTCOMES:

People—Frequently, these managers are well liked by a majority of their team while being silently despised by many of their high performers, who eventually leave for a more productive and supportive environment.

Manager—Pleaser managers often feel out of control and overwhelmed. The constant need to manage relationships without demonstrable results exacts its own toll with stress and ultimately, termination—if they are ever held accountable.

The Gamer

In the lower left quadrant you will find the manager who isn't trying to win and who doesn't build meaningful relationships with colleagues. We call them Gamers because without a connection to people or purpose, they spend their time playing a self-created game where status and survival are the score.

VALUES:

Gamer managers don't value confidence or humility and do not prioritize business results or relationships with colleagues.

FOCUS:

Gamers generally have a short-term focus on survival and status.

BEHAVIORS:

Gamers are manipulators. They spend their days playing dirty politics, working one person against another in their ceaseless quest for status. In their mind, winning is not related to organization results. Their meetings and efforts at delegation usually have two layers of meaning, with political subtext just beneath the surface.

OUTCOMES:

People—Gamers attract a motley cast of sycophants, other Gamers, and the disaffected. Productive employees leave as soon as they can.

Manager—In unhealthy organizations, Gamers can hang around a long time as they manipulate the people around them in a warped game of "who will be the last one voted off the island?" Whether or not a Gamer experiences stress and discomfort depends on his or her internal values. Living and working this way is caustic to people with any self-regard.

The Winner

Finally, in the upper right quadrant are the managers who win well.

VALUES:
Managers who win well bring confidence and humility in equal measure and focus on both results and relationships.

FOCUS:
Where the other three manager types tend to focus on short-term goals, managers who win well have a longer time horizon. They build teams that will produce results today as well as next year.

BEHAVIORS:
Managers who win well build healthy professional relationships with their employees. They maintain high expectations for results in a supportive environment where people can grow and take healthy risks. Managers who win well master the art of productive meetings, delegation, and problem solving. They run meetings that people consider a good use of time. These managers practice steady, calm accountability along with celebration.

OUTCOMES:
People—Their employees tend to stick around (often until they get promoted), and there is a line of people wanting to work for managers who win well.

Manager—They work with less overall stress than their colleagues and enjoy the benefits of productive, energized employees who take initiative and problem solve. These managers do work hard but tend to enjoy their work and have time to enjoy life outside of their job.

Where User and Pleaser managers can feel out of control and powerless over their circumstances, managers who win well know they have influence over their environment and enjoy a strong sense of personal responsibility and efficacy.

ONE WORD YOU CAN'T MANAGE WITHOUT

It's not easy to combine confidence and humility, and to focus on results and relationships. In fact, it is much easier to focus on differences. As human beings, we often think in terms of the word *or* rather than *and*. That's why you can find so many Users and Pleasers in the management ranks: They default to winning at all costs *or* being liked.

"Or" doesn't help you to thrive as a manager. In fact, reliance on "or thinking" is what causes most managers to become frustrated and bitter, and either quit or lose their soul at work. The real world is not an "or" world; it's an "and" world. The foundation of your success as a manager—the secret to begin Winning Well—is in this one word. The more you can use the "and," the more you will be able to win well and sustain excellent results over time. It's not about results or relationships, confidence or humility. The answer is in the "and"—you need all of them.

The real world is an "and" world. The more you use "and," the more you will be able to win well and sustain excellent results over time.

We want to conclude and demonstrate the power of the "and" with one of the most potent stories of confidence and humility that we've ever encountered.

Karin was conducting a workshop when Miomir, a tall, dark, handsome, and very confident Serbian shared a story that stopped her cold. Miomir said, "I've never seen anyone lead with confidence and humility during stressful times better than how my wife, Lori, led me to get my act together a few years ago."

Get his act together? This man oozed confidence and clearly stood out as one of the strongest leaders in the room. Everyone in the room encouraged him to explain.

"I was an absolute asshole. If you were to look up bad husbands in Wikipedia, my picture would be there. I had been such a jerk for so many months. I knew it. She knew it. I was deeply depressed, and not myself. We had no money, which made it even more difficult. She didn't complain. She never seemed to take it personally. That must have taken a huge amount of humility. She knew there was something going on with me, and instead of being mad about the impact I was having on her, she rallied her confidence to come up with a plan to help me figure it out.

"One day she asked: 'Would you be willing to fully trust me and get up at 3:00 a.m. with me tomorrow and follow me?'

"I felt so guilty that I said, 'Sure,' even though I found the mere thought exhausting. When she woke me up that morning, I rolled over. She kissed me and said, 'but you promised.' Confident and persistent, she blindfolded me—and took me skydiving, my top bucket-list adventure. We both knew we couldn't afford it, but I leaped in.

"As I felt myself falling, I pulled the cord and felt familiar joy begin swelling up inside of me. I recognized that guy, and I liked him.

"That night over a beer, my wife shared the videos and pictures she took. As she played them back, she reminded me, 'This is the man I love. This is who you really are. You can be this. You will get there again. I love you.'"

Lori was focused on results and relationships: She wanted a healthier husband and a stronger marriage. She was humble enough to see the situation was not about her and that her husband needed support, and was confident to take bold action.

Perhaps someone you're leading right now could use such a generous, humble, and confident approach. That's the power of the "and" as well as the foundation of being a manager who wins well.

Confidence and humility paired with a focus on results and relationships. When you approach every situation with these four characteristics, you vastly increase the odds of your own success, you will have more influence with other people, and you protect your soul against frustration, bitterness, and apathy.

YOUR WINNING WELL ACTION PLAN

To give you a snapshot of your management focus, values, and behaviors as well as a roadmap of how you can build on your strengths to win well, we've included a brief Winning Well Assessment (Figure 2.2). To complete the assessment, look at each pair of statements and mark the one that is more important to you. For each pair, choose only one of A or B.

FIGURE 2.2. THE WINNING WELL ASSESSMENT

Which is More Important, A or B?	
A	**B**
Putting out fires	Working long hours
Solving problems	Knowing things before anyone else
Being recognized	Building my status
Getting results	Being confident
Being liked by my employees	Achieving day-to-day goals
Working toward long-range goals	Keeping my job
Dealing with job-related stress	Not feeling frustrated
Being respected	Playing politics well

When you have marked one choice from all eight pairs, score the assessment:

Number of A's you selected: _____

Number of shaded A's you selected _____

Total of A's + shaded A's = _____

You should have a total number between 0 and 12. Look up your number on the following list of results.

Results

0-2 You probably experience lots of stress, bouncing back and forth between Gamer attempts to keep your job and frustration with your staff.

3 You likely do try to achieve results, but with a high degree of frustration common to the User style. You may try to be liked, but it generally doesn't work.

4 **(with no shaded A's)** You may identify with the Pleaser style, putting lots of effort into being liked and reacting to one crisis after another.

4 **(with 2 shaded A's)** You probably are a results-oriented manager with an opportunity to sustain your results as you connect with and invest in your people.

5 You have Winning Well management instincts that likely get buried in day-to-day stress and personnel frustrations.

6 **(with one shaded A)** You may identify with the Pleaser style, putting lots of effort into being liked and reacting to one crisis after another with some focus on results.

6 **(with three shaded A's)** You likely have Winning Well instincts and a focus on results.

7 You likely have Winning Well instincts and a focus on relationships.

8 You likely have strong Winning Well practices and may flex easily between results and relationships.

9-12 You likely have strong Winning Well practices and emphasize relationships in your day-to-day work.

This brief assessment gives you a small indication of your managerial style. For a more complete picture and full recommendations tailored to your style, we've included the full assessment online as part of your free Winning Well Tool Kit at www.WinningWellBook. com. We encourage you to complete the assessment and keep it beside you as you read the following chapters.

CHAPTER 3

Master the Metrics Maze

"Play to win and you will find yourself taking violent exercise; play because it is good for you and you will not."

—C. S. LEWIS, *OUR ENGLISH SYLLABUS*

Your customer doesn't care what you received on your internal scorecard. No employee can concentrate on 27 metrics at a time. Managers who win well pick a few meaningful measurements that encourage the right behaviors and make it tough to manipulate the stats just to get a short-term lift with no real improvement. They understand that the score is not the game. Most managers don't start here, however; instead, they drown in data and use it the wrong way.

• • •

Sarah winced as the hourly stack rankings beeped through her smartphone.

She didn't have to say a word. Karin knew that look from the inside out. She's been on the frantic receiving end of such beeps. Hourly results coming in 15 times a day—quality, efficiency, sales—all neatly ranked as a constant reminder that she wasn't doing

28

enough. And just in case the beeps didn't get her attention, at least one or two of the hourly blasts were typically followed up by a call from her boss: "Have you seen the numbers?"

Sarah interrupted Karin's painful flashback. "I'm sorry, but I've got to huddle the team. We've got to get to 94 by the end of the day."

"What are you planning as your key message?" Karin asked.

Sarah looked at her as if she was crazy. "Ninety-four," she said.

When Karin met with Sarah's team later in the day and asked what success looked like, she got more of the same.

"Ninety-four." Well, at least they were consistent.

When David taught high school, a week never went by without a student approaching him to ask, "Mr. Dye, what do I need to do to pass?"

Sometimes the question varied: "How can I get an 'A'?" "Can I get extra credit?" "My dad will kill me if I bring home a 'C'!" Despite all their stress and concern, students who asked these questions did not do as well as their peers.

These students share something in common with Sarah: They were focused on the score. The number, the grade, and the metrics—all of these are tools we use to evaluate what's happening. They tell you something about what's happened on the field, in the classroom, and in your business.

These metrics matter. A balanced scorecard, with well-selected key performance indicators, will reinforce your strategy and align actions with goals. We need them, and whether you like them or not, they're not going away.

But these measurements can also be a trap for many managers.

Imagine that you go to the doctor and are told that your blood pressure is high. The doctor prescribes a medication, change in diet, and more exercise. Assuming you are motivated to get healthy, what would you do when you leave the doctor's office?

You might go to a pharmacy, fill your prescription, and then head home. Once you got there, you might evaluate what food you have on hand and make a shopping list that includes whole grains, lean meats, and vegetables. You might take a walk and start an exercise plan.

Now imagine instead that you leave the doctor's office and first go to a medical supply store, pick up a blood pressure cuff, then head home and start taking your own blood pressure every 15 minutes. Your blood pressure is still high, and now you're stressed; you've got to achieve results! So you start taking your blood pressure every 10 minutes, only to see your blood pressure rise even higher.

We don't know any healthy people who have ever done this with their blood pressure, but when it comes to leading business teams, we see managers do it all the time. They focus on the score because they mistake the number for what it actually represents.

Your blood pressure score is not your blood pressure. The score is a set of numbers on a readout that tells you what's happening in your body. It is an indicator of health—it's not health itself.

If you're in law enforcement, the crime rate is an indicator of public safety, it's not public safety itself. If you're in sales, your average sale per customer is an indicator of your relationship with your customers, it's not the relationship itself. If you're in customer service, your service ratings are indicators, they're not the service itself.

Whatever measurements you use in your business, it's vital to understand that:

> *Measurements are not what you do;*
> *measurement represents what you do.*

USE DATA TO DRIVE, NOT DROWN, YOUR TEAM

There are four ways you can use data effectively:

1. Know what matters.

Your scores don't really matter. They are there to help you and your supervisors make decisions, but the scores . . . don't . . . matter.

What is truly significant? There is one surefire way to find out.

Ask: What does your customer or client care about?

Your customer doesn't care what grade your team received on your internal scorecard.

No one outside your team or your manager cares where you are in a ranking, how close you are to your goal, or what grade you got. They care about their results. For example:

- How long do they have to wait, and can they get their issues resolved to their satisfaction?

- Does your product work and meet their need the way they expect?

- Are they able to do what they expect when they use your service?

- Do they feel good about it?

- Does it help them?

Your team exists to produce those results. The results—what you do for your customers or clients—that's what matters. Focus on what matters most, and we guarantee your score will improve and you'll win well.

2. Know the key behaviors that produce real results.

If you wanted to lower your blood pressure, you would know your key behaviors: take your medicine, eat well, and exercise. Similarly, there are core sets of behaviors that allow your team to achieve results and sustain them over time.

If you're a nonprofit fund-raising director, your key behaviors might include:

- Build relationships with donors.

- Ask them to support the cause.

- Thank them in varied and meaningful ways.

If you're a convenience store retail manager, your key behaviors might include:

- Keep products stocked.

- Make sure the store is clean and neat.

- Don't let customers wait in a line longer than three people.

If you're a customer-service call-center supervisor, your key behaviors might include:

- Huddle with your team each day to connect and communicate.

- Listen to calls and provide balanced performance feedback.

- Get involved to help resolve the toughest customer concerns.

Whatever your business, there are always key behaviors that drive your meaningful results. Do you know yours? This is a critical step; you can't win, much less win well, if you don't know what drives your success.

3. Emphasize key behaviors (not the score).

As a manager, you keep the beat for the team. Everyone can play their parts when you keep time and anchor them in what really matters.

To keep the beat for your team, consistently emphasize the key behaviors. "This is how we succeed: We do A, B, and C." All your communication—in team meetings, in one-on-ones, in email—everything must emphasize these core practices.

When you do discuss metrics, put them in terms of the key behaviors. For example, "When we A, B, and C every day, we will be in the top 10 percent of the stack rank. We will get the revenue we need to serve our clients. We will maintain 80-percent-plus repeat visits."

4. Check the score at appropriate intervals.

How often should you check your metrics? The answer is: as often as necessary to keep you on track and no more than that.

In other words, it depends on what you're doing. Let's take two nonbusiness examples first:

If you're working to lower your blood pressure, checking it every day is probably too much. One day's reading doesn't give you much information. A monthly reading might be appropriate because it's the trend over time that tells you something meaningful.

However, if you're driving a convertible roadster down the highway, you probably need to glance at the speedometer every so often to make sure you don't get a ticket.

For your business, a good guideline is to think about how long it will take you to see results when you implement a change. If you make a change today, will you see results in a day? A week? A month? Six months?

Different businesses have different time frames. Generally, you want to check the score often enough to confirm positive results or to catch problems when something changes, but no more than that.

Why is this so important?

HOW FOCUSING ON THE SCORE DISTRACTS YOU FROM THE WIN

The score is not the game. When you focus too much on the score, you don't play the game—and bad things happen. The only real and lasting way to change the score is to play the game, not be a Gamer.

- Want a better blood pressure score? Take your medicine, eat well, and exercise.

- Want a better algebra grade? Learn how to solve the equations and do your homework.

- Want better business metrics? Identify the key behaviors that produce results and do those things consistently.

We know you've heard the stories of companies that focus on quarterly gains to please Wall Street and put off crucial long-term investments in technology, people, or infrastructure to sustain growth. Think about it this way: No coach has ever said, "We may have lost the game, but we owned the scoreboard for eight of nine innings!" To help you avoid these pitfalls, look for these five warning signs:

1. False sense of competition.

If, "We've got to beat Joe's team!" is a louder rally cry than, "Make a genuine connection with every customer!" you've missed the point and focused your team on a distraction, and your smack talk will backfire. It's time to regroup.

Competition can be healthy and productive. Compete to provide the best service. Work hard to offer the best product. Strive to offer the best experience you can—not to beat Joe. Your product, service, or experience is the real game.

2. Gaming.

Gerrymandering election districts, asking for extra-credit school assignments, and overreporting sales figures are all examples of gaming. Gaming refers to behaviors that change the score but aren't really about playing the game well. Gamers have no focus on real results.

We've seen astounding creativity in the huge lengths some employees and managers will go to to game the system. If they spent as much time improving the quality of their work as they spend working the work-around, they'd be knocking results out of the park.

When you exclusively focus on metrics, you encourage this kind of gaming. People will do what you ask them to do—in this case, to change the score. And they do it creatively, which wastes time, is often unethical, and gets people fired.

3. Volatile performance.

You can't respond to most metrics on an hourly (or even daily) basis. When you do, you're likely to be reactive and more annoying than helpful. When you're reactive, you exhaust your team and they will eventually ignore you.

If metrics go up when you rant, scream, or dress like a superhero, and then rapidly come down, take a step back and plan a consistent approach to reinforce key behaviors, again and again.

4. Unintended consequences.

If, "I fixed this, but broke that," sounds like the sad country music soundtrack of your group's performance, you're likely focused on one or two numbers rather than on the key game-changing behaviors that will lead to lasting performance.

In every business there are one or two vital behaviors that will improve your overall results. Be sure to focus on these early and often. Then build on that foundation.

5. Stupid decisions.

This happens at all levels but can be particularly disastrous when you become focused on a short-term adrenaline shot to force up results. "Oh sure, we can bring on 500 people in 10 weeks to get the contract," is not rational thinking. Focus your decisions on activities that lead to consistent upward trends and sustained performance. Respond with consistent improvement and celebrate upward trends, not flash-in-the-pan reactions to today's score.

You know you're Winning Well when employees are more proud of an actual customer experience or the difference they make in quality than of numbers on an Excel spreadsheet. Here's an example of where the employees cared so much they held themselves to a standard far more rigid than their scorecard measured.

• • •

Karin was brought in to help a call center that had grown and ventured into unknown territory. Its leaders knew its processes needed rigor, so they called her in to take a look and help them create a scalable model.

When she asked, "How do you measure performance?" there was an embarrassed silence followed by the awkward answer, "Attendance and adherence to schedule."

Now, you don't need to be a customer service genius to know that measuring whether or not reps show up to work is not enough to guarantee a great customer experience. Most centers at least use the Net Promoter Score, which measures whether the customer would recommend the company to a friend. But this project was different, and it wasn't so easy.

Her expectations lowered, Karin asked, "Would it be okay for me to sit with some reps?" And that's when the real surprise began.

She listened as the reps passionately explained their processes.

"Oh my gosh, I love my job, I just can't wait to help customers. You see this guy here? He thinks everything is fixed, but I dug a bit deeper, and I know we can help him more. It takes a few extra clicks to get what I need, but it's worth it."

"Well, each morning before I get to work, I go onto our—and our competitor's—Facebook page to see if anything hot might have surfaced since my last shift. Stuff changes fast, and it's important to come into work fully prepared."

"The best part of our work is that no one gives us a script; we are each able to use our own unique style as long as we follow the basic guidelines. Customers love that. We also share what works best with one another."

Then Karin reviewed customer conversations. She discovered that the company's scoreboard was irrelevant. These reps were scoring "10s" on an invisible scoreboard that tracked the intrinsic satisfaction they got from truly helping customers. Contrast their results-centered performance with the ubiquitous big-box retail cashier who hands you a receipt with a survey and tells you, "I will be punished if you give me anything less than a 10."

YOUR WINNING WELL ACTION PLAN

Identify the top three results your people are responsible for achieving. Now identify the results your customers or clients say are the three outcomes most important to them. Are these aligned?

1. What are the three most-important scores or metrics for your team or your business?

2. What are the top three core behaviors your team must perform to achieve meaningful results for your customers or clients?

3. Describe three ways you keep these behaviors (not only the metrics) consistently in front of your team.

Winning—

Achieve Results, Get Things Done, and Move to the Top

In this section you'll receive valuable tips, tactics, and tools you can use to achieve the results you need. These are tried-and-true practices that we've used throughout our careers and have shared with other managers to help them win well. They will make your life easier, improve morale, and distinguish you as a manager who gets things done with confidence and humility.

They include activities you do nearly every day: meet with people, delegate, make decisions, hold people accountable, and even remove someone from your team. It is hard to build genuine, healthy relationships with your people without these fundamentals. Get these right, however, and you're on your way to Winning Well.

CHAPTER 4

How to Keep Your People Focused on Results

"Gentlemen, what are your intentions?"
—CAPTAIN JIM LOVELL, *APOLLO 13*

We begin our discussion on results by offering specific techniques to increase your team's focus on what matters most, to recover from distractions, and to hold your team accountable.

• • •

The Apollo 13 mission suffered a major setback when an explosion damaged the spacecraft en route to the moon. The world watched as the astronauts tried to survive and return to Earth. If you've seen the eponymous 1995 film by Ron Howard, you might remember the scene where Captain Jim Lovell, played by Tom Hanks, asks the other astronauts, "Gentlemen, what are your intentions? Mine are to go home."

Lovell actually said this line, though the circumstances were slightly different from how the movie portrayed it. They were coming around from the far side of the moon and preparing a fuel burn to add momentum for the trip back to Earth. This was the first mission for the other two astronauts, Jack Swigert and Fred Haise, and they were busy taking pictures. Lovell called them back to the mission with his question and concluded by saying, "If we don't get home, you won't be able to have your pictures developed."[1]

Sometimes you will need to get your team back on track as Lovell did. Of course, another part of Winning Well is getting everyone on the same track in the first place. During a recent cross-country flight, Karin happened to sit next to an astronaut, Frederick Gregory, the former deputy administrator of the National Aeronautics and Space Administration who led the international management team for the International Space Station. They talked about leadership and what it takes to win well, and she asked him what it took for 14 diverse leaders from countries with tricky political dynamics to work together so successfully. He said:

"Hands down it's about focusing everyone on a common goal. Once we realized we all had the same big goal, we were able to get past the distraction of different opinions of how we should get there. We learned to release some of our preferred approaches and be open to other ways to accomplish our shared vision."

As an example, Gregory recounted that, "In order to get respect from the Russians, we first had to prove we could hold our own when it came to vodka. Once we proved that one night, we didn't need the vodka anymore and got to work."

Every manager experiences the challenge of distracted people or people pushing in different directions. Managers who lose their soul become frustrated with their team, blame them for their lack of focus, and punish people. However, like Lovell on the Apollo 13 mission, managers who win well are able to lead their people back to the mission and maintain their focus on results. How do they do it?

ACHIEVE REAL RESULTS WITH REAL PEOPLE

To keep your people focused on results, start with your own mindset. Managers who win well understand that people will be distracted. Many managers respond to this reality with frustration: "Hang on just a minute—these people are getting paid good money to stay focused. Surely I can expect that from them?"

Let's think about this for a moment. Those astronauts' very lives were at stake, and yet the beauty outside their window was irresistible. Even in dire circumstances, people can prioritize the less-immediate things.

You are in the fourth chapter of this book. How many times have you been distracted from your reading? How many interruptions have you faced? Have you diligently answered every Winning Well Action Plan question? We imagine you've had to set the book down and then refocus. Just like you, your people face many distractions every day. You can help reduce distractions and build a foundation for consistent results and healthy relationships by following these four steps.

1. Set Clear Expectations

We've found that roughly 90 percent of the problems managers have with poor performance result from deficiencies with this first step. No matter how clear your expectations are to you, it's likely they're not as clear to your people. When expectations are foggy, your people will lose focus and put their energy into other activities that make more sense to them. Of course, when they seem to slack off, your natural reaction is to get ticked off. Your reaction annoys your staff, who then wonder why you don't appreciate how hard they're working. And so the cycle continues.

Be clear and confident about what you expect and when it will be completed. In Chapters 5 and 9, we'll give you much more detail about how to do this in meetings as well as when you delegate. In the meantime, here is a quick and useful tool you can use to know for certain whether your people understand the expectations.

When you finish a discussion or share instructions, don't leave the conversation until you check for understanding. Here are several questions you can use:

❏ "Before we go, Joe, will you share what you understand the expectations to be?"

❏ "Joe, can you tell me what you heard?"

❏ "Let's review what we're doing next. What are the three steps we'll take today?"

❏ "Good discussion. Joe, can you tell us what are we doing today and tomorrow?"

Your goal is to get your people to share the steps, guidelines, agreement, actions, or expectations. You don't know that they know until you hear them say it.

You don't know that they know until
you hear them say it.

• • •

Dora was a district manager who took an area president, Steve, out to visit a distribution facility. This was his first visit to any of the centers in her district, so she needed to execute flawlessly.

The visit went well, and Steve made a number of excellent suggestions. Dora met with her local management team who had participated in the meeting and asked if they understood the suggestions. They said yes, and Dora asked them to put together an action plan. She would set up a call so they could review it the following week before sending it along to the president.

The next week, the management team joined the call, and Dora asked them to take her through the plan. There was complete silence on the other end of the phone. Finally, it came out: The managers thought they were going to build the plan on the call together. They'd done nothing and had lost an entire week. Dora had to assign extra resources to get it done quickly. The team was capable but did not understand what she had asked of them.

The problem was in her check for understanding. It's not enough to ask, "Do you understand?" Have your people repeat the expectations. When you check for understanding, your people might repeat back two action items but leave out a third. Then you can remind them. Or they might repeat all three but have the details wrong. The sooner you discover misaligned expectations, the faster you can clarify and get everyone pointed in the same direction.

2. Train and Equip People to Meet the Expectations

After unclear expectations, the next pitfall is to assume that everyone has the knowledge or skills to meet those expectations. Ensure that your team members are set up for success.

David once worked with a technology company whose bright engineers were creating cutting-edge technology that was used across the globe. As the company grew, it encountered communication challenges, missed deadlines, and frequent conflict as managers became upset with their people and one another.

Most of these problems stemmed from the fact that the engineers weren't using the scheduling software properly. The managers looked at their cadre of talented, smart engineers and assumed they wouldn't need to train the engineers in how to use the software. However, one button in the software wasn't immediately obvious to half the engineers, and as a consequence, they missed meetings, deadlines slipped, and tempers flared.

Be sure to train and equip people to meet expectations.

3. Reinforce Expectations

Effective managers continually reinforce expectations and keep clear priorities in front of their team, offering reminders where they're going and why. Your mind receives 11 million bits of information every second you are awake.[2] With that much information coming at your people, it can't hurt to say things twice. Your major strategic themes, objectives, and key priorities warrant repetition at least once every 28 days.

If your employees were a rock band, reinforcing expectations would be the drums or bass line that anchors the song and keeps everyone on track. It takes a consistent, steady, regular beat to keep your people focused.

4. Close the Loop with Celebration and Accountability

You've done all the hard work to ensure that expectations are clear and that people have the skills and equipment to meet the expectations, and you've consistently maintained everyone's focus. The next step is to maintain the momentum through celebration and accountability.

You can easily demotivate your team when you fail to celebrate success or practice accountability. Think of celebration and accountability as the final part of the expectation circle, the feedback that closes the loop and makes it likely your team will stay focused on what matters most.

When you don't close the results loop with feedback, you effectively tell your team their work doesn't matter. It doesn't matter if they did it right, and it doesn't matter if they did it wrong. When either result is usually met with silence, people ask, "What's the point?" and give up or move on.

Celebration can be as simple as calling your people together and privately acknowledging that they did it. In Chapter 20 we give you many more resources to celebrate and encourage your people. For now, when you celebrate, make sure the feedback you give is specific, meaningful to them, and relevant to the work and results. You'll get more of what you encourage and celebrate.

The word *accountability* isn't code for "beating people up when they don't perform." Think of *accountability* as "keeping our mutual agreements with one another." When we don't keep those agreements or fulfill our commitments, we need to talk about it. In Chapter 7 we share some tools to handle your accountability conversations well. In the meantime, sometimes all it takes is to call attention to an issue. You might say, "We agreed that we would do this, and we haven't. What happened and how can we get it done?"

Remember that your employees are human beings and even with the best intentions, good people can lose focus on results. It's your job to help them maintain a healthy focus on results with clear expectations, training to meet the expectations, consistent reinforcement of the expectations, and accountability with celebration.

YOUR WINNING WELL ACTION PLAN

Whenever you find yourself challenged with a management issue, we invite you to first ask these questions:

1. Are expectations clear to all parties? Check for understanding by asking your team to share the expectations. Visit the Winning Well website, www.WinningWellBook.com, to download an exercise that can help.

2. Does your team have the skills and equipment to succeed? (Don't guess—ask them.)

3. Have you consistently reinforced the expectations? Has it been more than 28 days?

4. Do you consistently practice accountability and celebration? When was the last time you offered a sincere, "Congratulations" or, "We need to do better"?

NOTES

1. Jim Lovell and Jeffrey Kluger, *Lost Moon: The Perilous Voyage of Apollo 13* (New York: Houghton Mifflin, 1994), 240.

2. *Encyclopaedia Britannica Online*, "Information Theory," by George Markowsky, accessed June 15, 2015, http://www.britannica.com/EBchecked/topic/287907/information-theory/214958/Physiology.

CHAPTER 5

Lead Meetings That Get Results and That People Want to Attend

---

"The meeting of two personalities is like the contact of two chemical substances: if there is any reaction, both are transformed."

—CARL JUNG

Horrible meetings are a cliché of the business world, and with good reason. Many meetings are a waste of time and don't accomplish anything. The minutes creep along while the meeting leader fritters away everyone's time, people have meaningless conversations that don't solve problems, and everyone is frustrated that they could be doing something more productive with their time. When you don't run meetings well, not only do your results suffer, so does your credibility. In this chapter, you will learn some specific techniques for running more efficient and productive meetings that improve results and relationships.

• • •

Even though we love to hate meetings, you cannot achieve results without bringing people together to make decisions and take action, whether in person, online, or on a conference call. You may be the most skillful, competent surgeon, engineer, customer service rep, finance manager, nurse, or salesperson the world has ever known, but when you can't lead meetings your credibility evaporates.

Conference calls can be a similar soul-sucking waste of time. Somehow we think that a conference call will save time. In fact, it's that kind of thinking that leaves many managers moving from call to call with little time to connect with their team. In an attempt to get a little something done, they put the phone on mute and try to get real work done at the same time—and don't pay close attention to much as a result.

What are your meetings like? Consider the last meeting you facilitated, whether in person, online, or by phone. Would you have more promoters or detractors? What would each of these groups say on their way out the door?

Promoters

- "The meeting had a clear purpose and agenda."

- "All the right people were there."

- "Everyone contributed."

- "We stayed right on topic."

- "We made lots of decisions."

- "I know just what to do next."

Detractors

- "It was more of a one-way information dump."

- "I am not really sure what that meeting was about."

- "The right people weren't there."

- "We didn't stay on topic."

- "We didn't make any decisions."

- "We were just there to update our boss."

If you think you would have heard more from the detractors list than the promoters list, it's time to make your meetings productive, meaningful, and something people want to attend.

Let's begin with one of the biggest reasons people hate meetings. They abuse our most precious resource: time.

DON'T WASTE MY TIME

Effective managers treat everyone's time as a precious resource. When you value someone's time, you show great respect for another human being. In contrast, when you carelessly let meetings run long, or start late, or have a meeting you never should have called, you disrespect your people.

The first thing you can do to make meetings work for you and your team is to hold meetings only when they are the most valuable use of all the attendees' time. If there is something employees could do that is more valuable, that contributes more directly to the team and to the results you're trying to accomplish, why on earth would you want them in your meeting where they are less productive?

So how do you make sure a meeting is a good use of time? It starts with purpose. Every meeting you hold should accomplish two goals that will sound familiar: build relationships and achieve results.

Teams require trust, and that is built only through time spent together, through solving problems, making decisions, and learning how everyone operates, sees the world, and shares information. In addition to the connections built through working together and solving problems, you can also include periodic conversations that build relationships, such as:

- Cultural conversations to problem solve or celebrate: for example, "What's really getting in the way of people using our new system?" or, "What have you seen another member do well over the last month?"

- Elephant-in-the-room conversations: for example, "What are the conversations we're not having that we should be having?"

- Mutual-help conversations: for example, "Let's talk about how we're working with other departments. What's working well? Where do we have challenges?" Give people a chance to share and help one another.

These conversations can happen quickly and be a rich source of positive relationships and results as your people learn to trust each other and help one another.

Your meetings should also move the mission of your group, team, and organization forward. In short, meetings should produce action. You got together to solve a problem, make a decision, or share information, and when the meeting ends, it's time to do something. If your meetings don't result in clear action, you've wasted your time.

We're not saying you should never hold a meeting. Effective teams meet frequently. You want to be certain the meetings you hold are effective and that they are the best use of every attendee's time. This will happen when you focus every meeting to build relationships and achieve results. If your meeting isn't going to build relationships and advance the mission of the organization, don't have the meeting.

GET THE RIGHT PEOPLE IN THE ROOM

Who should attend a meeting? You want the smallest number of stakeholders that will allow you to make the best decision. Think about the number of people in your meeting as a continuum. On one end, you could hold the meeting with just yourself. It might look funny, but you could sit there by yourself, examine what you know, make a decision, and then share the decision with everyone else.

On the other end of the continuum, you could have everyone—every single person in the organization—attend a meeting. If you have a 50-person organization, all 50 of them would attend, and that would be unwieldy, but if you work in a 10,000-person organization, it would be impossible. So the question is, what is the smallest number of people who can attend but still provide you with good, diverse, and informed input from those who have a stake in the decision?

Where most leaders go wrong is that they invite too many people who have the same perspective and fail to invite key representatives with different vantage points who might help them make a better decision if they had input.

In business, if two men agree,
one of them is unnecessary.

—William Wrigley Jr.

Remember, the goal of the meeting is to take action. When you take people away from their normal work, you do it so that all of you together can make a better decision than you would have done on your own. You'll waste everyone's time if you don't invite the necessary people to the meeting.

WHY ARE WE HERE?

Next, you want to be clear about what kind of meeting you're holding. There are several types of meetings, but we're going to focus on the two most common ones.

The first type is the informational meeting. These are short meetings to exchange information. The key for an informational meeting is that there is an exchange of information (not just information going in one direction). It's not you pulling people together because it's more convenient for you. Remember, the meeting needs to be the most valuable use of their time as well. This can happen if there is an honest exchange, an opportunity to ask questions, and interaction around the information being shared, and the meeting is brief.

The second type of meeting exists to make decisions and take action. Most of your meetings should fall into this category. They can be anywhere from 15 minutes to two hours long and feature a specific decision to make or a problem to solve (a problem is just a specific kind of decision). In his book *Death by Meeting*, Pat Lencioni says that the heart of a good meeting is "drama"—that there is some kind of conflict worth discussing.[1]

The key to make meetings work for you and your team is to be very clear about what kind of meeting you've called. When you mix up an information exchange with decision making, it frustrates everyone. If you want to solve a specific problem, don't allow a team member to turn the meeting into a briefing on her latest project unless it specifically helps the group solve the problem at hand. Stay focused on the specific objectives for the meeting you're leading.

So far you've ensured that the purpose of your meeting is to build relationships and achieve results, you'll get the least number of people it will take to produce the best outcome, and you're clear about the kind of meeting you've scheduled. Now it's time to make sure those decision-making meetings are productive.

WINNING WELL MEETING FORMULA

Does this sound familiar? You went to a meeting where you had invigorating discussions, examined alternatives, and came up with a cool plan of action; everyone left the meeting feeling motivated, and then six weeks later you got back together. As everyone entered the room and took their seat, there were sideways glances.

"Did you do that thing we talked about?"

"No, how about you?"

A quick shake of the head and you realized that the great idea everyone talked about had languished.

The prior meeting, the discussions, the new meeting—all of it—were a waste because nothing happened. In fact, it's worse than doing nothing because now you've created negative energy, that feeling that, "It doesn't matter what we talk about because nothing really changes around here."

That corrosive malaise will eat away at your people until you have a group of zombies shuffling through their day without any meaning or purpose to their work. Every manager we've ever worked with has experienced this frustrating lack of follow-through after decisions are made. It can even happen with a team of high-caliber, motivated people who take their work seriously.

Every meeting you hold should produce activities that move results forward, build momentum, and build morale with healthy relationships. You can achieve all this in just five to ten minutes at the end of every meeting.

Let's begin with mindset. We invite you to think about meetings as commitment creators. In other words, the outcome for every decision-making or problem-solving meeting you ever have is to create commitment. You get the right people together to discuss the problem, you make a decision, and people commit to do something. The product of a good meeting is a commitment to activity. You build this commitment with three questions.

Commitment 1: Who Will Do What?

Until someone actually does something, nothing has changed from before you made the decision. Until then, it is just a nice idea.

There are actually two questions here:

What is to be done?

Who will do it?

We prefer to combine them into one question because it guarantees ownership. Every task must have a specific person who is responsible to complete it. For smaller decisions there might be only one or two answers to this question. For larger, strategic initiatives you might have an entire work plan that outlines dozens of tasks and people responsible.

Commitment 2: By When?

This one is straightforward. What is the finish line for the tasks people have agreed to complete? When these deadlines are shared and publicly available, everyone is more likely to meet them.

Commitment 3: How Will We Know?

Pablo shrugged, "Linda, I did those updates. I don't see why you're so upset."

Linda's team had decided to launch a new product that involved many moving parts. They had clearly answered the first two questions: Who does what and by when? For the most part, everyone kept to their commitments, and yet the delivery date kept slipping.

When Linda investigated, she discovered that individuals had done what they'd said they would do, but there was still something missing. Linda and other team members couldn't always take the next step until another person had finished her piece. Pablo had finished his piece but never let anyone else know. He had moved onto other work, diligently crossing items off his to-do list while the overall project sat idle.

In big projects you may have a project manager or a project management tool to ensure that this type of next-step communication happens, but what about in your more ordinary, day-to-day meetings? Where is the accountability?

"How will we know?" is the magic question that moves your meeting from good intentions to real-world impact. It's also the one managers most frequently ignore. "How will we know?" closes the loop from intention to action and creates momentum without you having to spend hours every day tracking down action steps. Here's how it works: When someone completes a task, what does he do next?

- Does he need to pass the results to another person or group?

- Should he update the team and let them know?

- Will he make a presentation of his findings?

- Does he report completion in a common area or software?

The specific answers depend on the task and project. What matters is that the accountability and next step are baked into the decision. Everyone knows what he or she is accountable to do, the team knows if it's been completed, and no one is left waiting around for information she needs.

Combine these commitments into one sentence—Who does what, by when, and how will we know?—and you have the Winning Well Meeting Formula to get clarity, accountability, and results in just five minutes at the end of every meeting: In fact, you can ask these questions whether you are the positional leader of a group or not. That's a great way to establish yourself as a leader who gets things done; people notice when you produce clarity, accountability, and results. Don't let the simplicity of these questions fool you into not using them. We've seen thousands of managers struggle and get frustrated because they didn't ensure this kind of clarity at the end of every meeting. These are the most important five minutes you'll spend to make your meetings achieve results.

YOUR WINNING WELL ACTION PLAN

Before scheduling your next meeting, consider:

1. Is this meeting the best use of time for the people you will invite?

2. Will this meeting build relationships and achieve results?

3. What kind of meeting is this (information exchange, make a decision, or solve a problem)?

4. Have you scheduled time at the end of the meeting to complete the Winning Well Meeting Formula: Who will do what, by when, and how will you know?

NOTES

1. Pat Lencioni, *Death by Meeting* (San Francisco: Jossey-Bass, 2004), 226.

CHAPTER 6

How to Make Business Decisions Your People Get Behind

"I am heartened to find so much wit in you, that you'd give thought to consequences and choose your way with reason, not passion only."

—DEBORAH LIGHTFOOT, *THE WYSARD*

Next we turn to the important topic of decision making. Winning Well managers are clear on how the decision will be made and who is involved, erring on the side of inclusion whenever possible.

• • •

"This is so stupid—you asked for my opinion and then ignored it. I don't know why I even bother! From now on, I'm just going to shut my mouth and do my work."

We've both heard these words and so has nearly every manager we've ever worked with. You may even have been the one to say them. This kind of frustration and anger reflects a broken decision-making process and goes far beyond one upset employee. In this chapter we show you why this happens and how to fix it.

WORK WITH HUMAN NATURE

Many managers struggle with frustration, bitterness, and loss of soul because they engage in a hopeless war with human nature by ignoring people's need to be included in discussions about where they are going, why they are going there, and how they will get there.

The truth is that most people will work with a decision when they are clear about what is required and why the decision was made, and if they had input into the decision. It doesn't mean they have to love it. They're adults and don't expect that every single decision will go their way. They do want to know that their information, values, and perspective were taken into consideration

You will always come out ahead when you work with human nature, not against it. It takes less time, is easier in many ways, and is more sustainable—you can keep it up for years without burning out.

As you saw in Chapter 5, one of the most common types of meetings you hold is the meeting to make a decision. If you want your team to win, you've got build their decision-making expertise. However, in companies we work with, from global multinationals to four-person start-ups in industries ranging from hardware engineering to nonprofit human service, we consistently see ineffective decision making lead to manager frustration, poor employee engagement, and general organizational dysfunction.

You can't afford to have your people retreat from decisions; you need their input to ensure that the best decisions are made and so they have buy-in for implementation. In our experience, most management training overlooks this skill. That's sad, because with just a few key practices added to your meeting checklist, you can save yourself weeks or months of lost time and frustration while also increasing employee engagement. In fact, there are just two critical pieces of information you need to introduce at the start of your discussion:

1. What kind of decision is this?

2. Who owns the decision?

WHAT KIND OF DECISION IS THIS?

The first step to making decisions that everyone gets behind is to make just one decision at a time and limit discussion to that single decision. We see teams waste precious hours and weeks arguing about the wrong things. Everything else is either better discussed individually (for instance, how an individual is going to tackle a project or what kind of training he will receive) or isn't a decision at all (for instance, a personal discussion reconciling a relationship after someone has let you down). The good news here is that there are only two types of business decisions to make.

The first type is a decision about goals: Where are we going? For example, a space agency might discuss whether to colonize the moon, travel to Mars, or stay home and focus on the Earth. The question, "Where are we going?" can take many forms, but it's always about your group's goal, destination, or outcome. Other ways to ask this question are, "What is the outcome we need to achieve?" or, "What does success look like?"

You can't talk about how you're going to do those things until you've first clearly decided what success looks like. Know where you are going before you discuss how to get there.

The second type of decision is: How will we get there? This is a discussion about methods.

For example, if the decision has been made to go to Mars, "How will we get there?" might be a discussion of whether to use private spacecraft or government ships. Or whether this will this be a one-way trip or a return mission.

Separate discussions about where you are going from how you will get there. Managers get in trouble when they allow these discussions to get mixed up. The team starts out talking about whether to go to the moon, to Mars, or focus on Earth, and 30 minutes later they're discussing the benefits of private versus public funding, then a few minutes later they're arguing about where they might land on the moon. The discussion is confused, perplexing, and wastes time because the question isn't clear.

WHO OWNS THE DECISION?

Let's return to the upset employee we quoted at the beginning of the chapter: "This is so stupid—you asked for my opinion and then ignored it. I don't know why I even bother! From now on, I'm just going to shut my mouth and do my work."

If you've heard this or said it yourself, you've experienced the second decision-making mistake managers commit: lack of clarity around decision ownership.

People hate feeling ignored. Unfortunately, when you ask for input and appear to ignore it, employees feel frustrated, devalued, and powerless. In contrast, when you are clear about who owns the decision and how it will be made, people will readily contribute and are far more likely to own the outcome.

This isn't difficult, because there are only four ways to make a decision:

1. A single person makes the decision.

Typically, this would be the manager or someone she appoints. In this style of decision making, you might ask your team for input and let them know that after hearing everyone's perspective, you will make the decision.

2. A group makes the decision through a vote.

This might be a 50-percent-plus-one majority or a two-thirds majority, but in any case, it's a decision by vote. With this option, you ask everyone to contribute input, and they know that the decision will be made by a vote at a specific time.

3. A team makes the decision through consensus.

Consensus is often misunderstood. Consensus decision making means that the group continues discussion until everyone can live with a decision. It does not mean everyone got his or her first choice, but that everyone can live with the final decision. Consensus decision making can take more time and often increases everyone's ownership of the final decision.

4. Fate decides.

You can flip a coin, roll the dice, draw from a hat, etc. There are times where flipping a coin is the most efficient way to make a decision. When time is of the essence, the stakes are low, and pro-con lists are evenly matched, it's often good to just pick an option and go. For example, if you have 45 minutes for a team lunch, it doesn't make any sense to spend 30 minutes discussing options. Narrow it down to a few places, flip a coin, and go.

• • •

Each way of deciding has advantages, but what's most important is to be very clear about who owns the decision.

When that person said, "You asked for my opinion and then ignored it. I don't know why I even bother!" he was under the impression that the team would decide by vote or consensus when in reality it was the leader's decision. This type of confusion wastes tons of precious time and energy and sucks the soul from your team.

Before discussion begins, state how the decision will be made. You get yourself in trouble (not to mention that it's unfair, disempowering, and quite soulless) if you suggest a vote and then change back to "I'll decide" when you think the vote won't go your way.

Before discussion begins, be clear about who owns the decisions. How will this decision be made?

Be specific. For example, you might begin a decision-making session by saying, "Okay, I'd like to spend the next 40 minutes getting everyone's input, and then I'll make the decision." Or, you might describe the decision to be made and say, "We're not going to move forward until everyone can live with the decision."

You might even combine methods and say, "We will discuss this decision for 30 minutes. If we can come to a consensus by then, that would be great. If not, we'll give it another 15 minutes. After that, if we don't have consensus, I'll take a final round of feedback and I'll choose, or we'll vote."

You save yourself grief, misunderstanding, and hurt feelings when everyone knows up front how the decision will be made. You also empower your people to be more influential because when they know who owns the decision, they also know how to share their information. Do they need to persuade the single decision maker, a majority, or the entire team? They can choose their most relevant information and arguments.

YOUR WINNING WELL ACTION PLAN

Think about the next decision you will make with your employees.

1. What kind of decision will this be: Where are you going, or How will you get there?

2. Who owns the decisions: you, the team through a vote, or the team through consensus?

3. When the decision is made, use the Winning Well Meeting Formula to clarify who does what, by when, and how you will know.

Think about a decision where you will participate but will not lead the meeting.

1. Can you articulate what kind of decision the group will make? If not, how can you ask for clarity?

2. Is it clear who owns the decisions? If not, what specifically can you do to gain clarity?

CHAPTER 7

How to Hold Your People Accountable Without Losing Your Soul

"Human kindness has never weakened the stamina or softened the fiber of a free people. A nation does not have to be cruel to be tough."

—FRANKLIN D. ROOSEVELT

Have you ever found yourself reluctant to hold an employee accountable because you were worried he'd leave? Or let a performance issue fester for fear of not being liked? In this chapter we address the challenging process of holding people accountable without coming across as a jerk.

• • •

David found himself in the middle of this dilemma when he opened a crinkly onionskin paper one of his volunteers had just handed him. He led a group of volunteers who contributed their time to work with disadvantaged children. One of these volunteers, Joanne, was a retired English teacher. She had typed a letter that grabbed his attention.

"David, thank you for the opportunity to volunteer; however, I would like to reevaluate my service at your school."

David had fallen into a common management trap. He had not provided enough structure or accountability because he was worried about losing bodies. The problem is that when you let expectations slide, when you tolerate poor performance, when you allow abuse, you tell everyone else that you don't care. Letting slackers slide reduces your credibility, causes your best performers to bolt, and leaves the rest of the team wondering why they bother. High performers hate nothing more than watching their poor-performing, soul-sucking teammates drag down results. That was Joanne's message: Don't waste my time or my work. Tolerating poor performance creates a morale death spiral that takes Herculean force to reverse.

Then there's the over-the-cube talk about the two slackers—the guy performing poorly *and you*. The more you allow the poor performance to go on, the more the rest of the team will shrug their shoulders and either join the poor-performance bandwagon or leave for somewhere that appreciates their effort. The death spiral accelerates, squanders time, and drains vital energy from your team.

Remember from Chapter 4 that our definition of accountability is not beating someone up for poor performance but keeping your mutual commitments to one another. This goes both ways: Managers who win well encourage their employees to hold them accountable for their commitments. A Winning Well accountability mindset brings results and relationships into laser-like focus.

The sad truth is that every day, team leaders around the world turn their heads and let the poor performance continue. Avoid these traps.

WHY TEAM LEADERS TOLERATE POOR PERFORMANCE

Here's a gut check if this is hard for you and you tolerate poor performance from your employees. See if any of these mistakes sound familiar.

❏ **Unclear Expectations.** You haven't done the work to be clear about what success looks like. When you get frustrated with your poor performers, they get frustrated with you, so you shut down and things don't change. Start with the fundamentals. Review Chapter 4 and clarify expectations. You can't practice accountability without mutual commitments about what should happen.

❏ **Guilt.** You worry you haven't done enough to support, develop, encourage, build confidence in, empower, or recognize an employee. If that's truly the case, you're right—you have more work to do. But if you have invested in the employee, invested again, and it's still not working, it's time to face the facts: This job may not be the right fit for the employee. Stop feeling guilty. You need to do what's right for the greater good of the company, the team, and the person.

❏ **False Morale.** We've seen many managers, mostly Pleasers, worried about building great morale who actually destroy it. If everything everyone does is "just great" then the folks who really give their all wonder why they do. We can't tell you how many times we've had the rest of the team thank us for addressing poor performance. Of course, such things are private, but your team is more astute than you may think.

❏ **Saving Face.** You hired the guy. Perhaps you even convinced your boss that he was "the one." If you've done everything you can to make it work, but it isn't going well, it's far better to admit you were wrong, learn from your experience, and move on. Don't magnify one poor decision with another.

❏ **Fear.** You're scared. You're not sure how to approach the situation. There's often nothing harder to do than to address poor performance or remove someone from the team. It never is easy, but it does get easier. Practice your conversation with a peer or mentor. Use the INSPIRE method we share later in this chapter. Plan the conversation, anticipate, and prepare for responses.

❏ **Lack of Alternatives.** Karin can recall countless times in her corporate job when someone called her for an internal reference on a poor performer whom they were about to hire, and after she shared the issues and concerns, the person was hired anyway. One person actually told her, "Well, Karin, you have very high standards. I'm not sure that's realistic." Hire slowly. The great ones are out there and deserve a chance.

If you have a struggling performer on your team, do all you can to help. And if it's time to let the person move on, help her do it gracefully (see Chapter 11 on how to terminate with grace and dignity).

Set high standards and serve your people. Results will follow. Don't give up. We've seen too many Pleaser managers give in and lower their standards to be nice, or Users reactively take a no-more-mister-nice-guy approach when results don't move quickly. Create the balance and stay the course.

INSPIRE ACCOUNTABILITY METHOD

Winning Well managers approach accountability conversations with a clear plan that will build relationships and achieve results. Your overall goals in these conversations are to:

1. Draw attention to the performance issues

2. Have a mutual discussion

3. Confirm commitment to new behavior

Use the INSPIRE method to achieve these goals with a short, to-the-point, specific conversation about what must change.

I—Initiate

Initiate the conversation in a respectful manner. Traditional feedback models often start with the person giving the feedback asking for permission. For example, you might ask a colleague, "Can we talk about what happened this morning?" Feedback is best received when you've been welcomed to provide it. Most of the time that's an awesome start. Sometimes, though, the conversation isn't optional. You may need to be more direct. Even in those instances, you can establish respect. For example, you might say, "I need to talk with you today. Is this a convenient time or would you prefer this afternoon?" Initiate accountability conversations as close to the moment of concern as possible. Don't wait three days to address something that happened this morning. Take care of it at the first opportunity.

N—Notice

Share your concern or observation.

- "I've noticed there are paint drips on the floor when you leave a job."

- "In listening to your calls, I've noticed you don't connect with the customer."

- "I noticed that you arrived late this morning."

S—Specific Support

Provide specific, supporting evidence you can see.

- "In the last two homes you painted, there were splatters on the hardwood in the dining room and on the rug in the baby's room."

- "When the customer told you he was calling to disconnect his line because his spouse had died, you didn't express any empathy. You said you would be happy to disconnect the line."

- "The meeting was scheduled for 9:00, and you arrived at 9:30."

P—Probe

After you present the situation, the employee needs a chance to talk. Ask a question in a neutral, curious tone to allow her to share any relevant information. Generally, "What happened?" is adequate and allows the person to share information or to own the situation.

- "What happened in those rooms?"
- "What happened on that call?"
- "What happened that you were late?"

Occasionally there will be an understandable reason for the poor performance. For example, the person may have been late because of a car accident. If so, be sure she's okay and don't carry the conversation any further.

I—Invite

Once he's had a chance to share his thoughts, invite him to solve the problem. Start with a review of the expectations, then ask for his thoughts on how to resolve the issue. Usually, this will be straightforward. For example, "I'll use a drop cloth and do a final inspection before leaving the property."

If he can't come up with an effective solution, you can provide specific suggestions on how the employee could improve.

- "Please put down a drop cloth every time you paint. You should also use masking tape to protect the molding from drips."

- "I suggest you take a moment to listen to what the customer is really saying, ask yourself what emotion he's shared, pause, and use an empathy statement before you jump right into action."

- "Give yourself 30 minutes for a client call before your next appointment."

Sometimes you may discover that the employee needs more training. For instance, Tito had been late to a team meeting. In the Probe stage, it came out that Tito had to pass by the CEO's office on the way to the meeting. Tito had responsibility for a project of special concern to the CEO and got pulled into conversation because he didn't know how to say no. In these situations, clarify the expectation and give the employee the tools to meet it. For example, "When the CEO asks if you have a minute, you might tell her that you're on your way to a meeting and ask if she would mind if you came back to brief her at 10:00 a.m. Let's practice...."

R—Review

Ask one or two open-ended questions to check for understanding and one closed-ended question to secure commitment.

- "How would your results be better if you did that every time?"

- "What concerns do you have about this approach?"

- "Is this your commitment going forward?"

Ask the employee to review her specific commitment: "Would you please recap what you will do next time?"

E—Enforce

Enforce the behavior and why it's important while reinforcing your confidence that the employee can do this.

- "Clean homes and use of a drop cloth are fundamental requirements of this job. In order for you to continue in this position you need to do a quality job."

- "I'll check back with you on your next three calls and look for those empathy statements and customer connection."

- "I'll see you at 9:00 a.m. for the next meeting. You are an important member of the team, and we don't make the best decisions without you."

You might conclude with:

- "I have every confidence you can do this well."

- "I appreciate your taking the time to make this happen."

- "Thank you for your work and commitment."

When behavior doesn't change, it's often because the feedback is too vague, or the conversation goes so long that the employee forgets what he needs to do. Work to INSPIRE specific behavior change with brief accountability conversations.

THE FINAL INGREDIENT

Claire, a gruff Midwesterner who managed an organization of environmental health and safety contractors, wiped an uncharacteristic tear from her eye. "Expectations are clear, I've had accountability conversations, and things got better . . . for a while. But now we're right back where we were, and I don't know what to do."

As we explored the situation, we discovered that Claire had done a good job clarifying expectations and would then have an accountability conversation with an employee who didn't do the work properly. So far so good—but then she stopped. In a few weeks, the employees returned to their prior habits.

We asked Claire about one particular employee. "Well, we talked and he did it right for a couple weeks. Then he had three weeks where he didn't."

"And did you speak with him about those three weeks?"

"Well, no." Claire sighed, "I'm not his mom."

Claire's situation isn't unique. Many managers struggle with consistent performance because they don't practice consistent accountability. Claire didn't want the guilt. For Pleaser managers, the work of follow-up isn't fun and conflicts with their desire to be liked. User managers often neglect consistency because it feels tedious or like too much effort away from direct results. Regardless of the reason, inconsistent accountability won't work.

It usually takes several moments to reinforce a pattern. These accountability moments might be with one employee or spread across several of them. When they see consistent expectations reinforced consistently, those expectations will become the norm. However, when you maintain expectations only every once in a while, you silently communicate that it's okay not to perform, as long as they don't mind an occasional mild slap on the hand. Managers who win well practice consistent accountability.

YOUR WINNING WELL ACTION PLAN

1. Are there areas of poor performance that you have tolerated? If so, reflect on one of those situations and ask:

   a. What keeps you from practicing accountability (unclear expectations, guilt, concern for morale, saving face, lack of confidence, no alternatives)? How can you reframe or address this issue?

   b. How can you use the INSPIRE method to plan your conversation with the employee?

2. Think back to managers who have held you accountable. What did they do well that you appreciated? How can you integrate those practices into your accountability conversations?

3. Go to www.WinningWellBook.com and download our confidence-competence worksheet to help you get to the root cause of accountability problems.

4. Schedule accountability check-ins. If you're working with an employee on a specific behavior, schedule a regular time on your calendar to check in with him or her on how it's going. If it's going great, use that time to recognize the behavior. If not, use that as an opportunity for further coaching and documentation.

CHAPTER 8

How to Solve the Right Problem Quickly and Get Back to Work

> *"No good manager needs to be convinced that problem analysis and decision making are the most important things he does. . . . Success virtually depends on doing these things well."*
>
> **—CHARLES KEPNER AND BENJAMIN TREGOE,**
> *THE RATIONAL MANAGER*

The difference between average and exceptional managers who win well often comes down to how well they solve problems. When obstacles arise that keep you and your people from achieving results, what do you do? When someone walks up to you and says, "Can I talk to you a minute—we've got a problem," how do you respond? How do you determine if you should be directly involved in solving the problem or if an employee should try first?

When confronted with problems, User Managers tend to get frustrated and lash out at their people while Pleaser Managers erratically search for answers that will get their boss or customer off their back. Winning Well managers take responsibility for solving problems. They determine the best person to own the problem and work to resolve it there. Use the following tips to quickly solve problems and get back to work.

• • •

Poncha was a respected nurse manager who treated her staff well, ran an efficient unit, and was good with patients. However, her staff was upset because patient satisfaction scores had declined over the past two months. After a little digging, Poncha tracked down the relatively minor issue: Patients were cold. Frank, the manager responsible for inventory and equipment, wasn't getting the blankets washed and distributed every morning.

This was clearly a part of his job description, but when Poncha spoke with him about the issue, she discovered that the surgery center administrator, Don, whom they both reported to, had given Frank other priorities for his early morning work. Frank was a Pleaser Manager type and didn't want to question his boss.

Poncha and her employees were being held accountable for the consequences of a problem they could not directly solve. These kinds of inefficiencies and potential conflicts happen in every organization; a decision by one person affects the results and welfare of employees in unforeseen ways. This reality of organizational life can frustrate even the most unflappable managers.

Poncha let Frank know she would be speaking with Don and invited him to come along. When they had the conversation, Poncha framed the issue in terms that resonated with Don. "We have an issue that can negatively impact revenue by 5 to 10 percent over the next six months." Once she captured Don's attention, she was able to explain the situation and propose solutions. Don agreed, Frank was happy to do what he was told to do, and the patients got their blankets.

Poncha demonstrated the first Winning Well problem-solving tip: Take responsibility without owning other people's problems. When you take responsibility, you ask, "How can I make this better?" Then you determine who actually owns the problem. In this case, Frank could have owned the problem, but it wasn't Poncha's job to change Frank (she didn't own someone else's problem). When she asked herself, "How can I make this better?" it was clear that she needed to talk with Don. She took responsibility, located the problem with its proper owner, phrased the problem in terms that were meaningful to the person who owned it, and shared possible solutions.

FIND THE REAL PROBLEM

You can waste incredible amounts of time in vain attempts to solve the wrong problem. Managers who win well don't leap in with solutions right away. When they are presented with a problem, they pause, ask questions, and work to identify the real issue.

Imagine if, when Poncha first heard that her nurses were upset, she had immediately responded the way many managers react to problems, saying something like, "Satisfaction scores are down? All right, let's work on that—move faster, be nicer!" Her "solution" would frustrate her staff and mask the actual problem. Scores might even briefly improve, but they would not be sustainable. When presented with a problem, avoid the inclination to react immediately.

What people bring to you is likely a symptom of the problem, not the problem itself. Pause. Get curious. Ask questions. Get the relevant facts. Here are three specific questions you can ask to help identify the real problem and not waste valuable time addressing symptoms:

1. What is different than expected?

In *The Rational Manager*, Charles Kepner and Benjamin Tregoe define a problem as "a deviation from some standard of performance."[1] Simply put, what didn't go the way you expected? When Poncha asked, "What is different than expected?" it was obvious that the overall patient satisfaction scores were lower than they had expected.

2. What has not changed?

This is a critical step that most managers skip altogether. When you identify a problem, it is helpful to know what has not changed. This helps eliminate issues that needn't concern you. For example, when Poncha understood that scores had dropped, she asked,

"Which scores? Is it all of them or just a few?" As she examined the data, it became clear that most of the scores had held steady and just those around comfort had changed. This helped her narrow her problem solving. The issue was not speed or quality of care, but comfort.

3. Why? Why? Why?

Once you've limited the problem to what it is and what it is not, look for causes by asking, "Why?" You will often have to ask several times. Poncha asked, "Why have patient comfort scores declined over the past two months?"

When she asked the staff for their thoughts, no one could come up with an answer that fit the problem (changes that only impacted comfort and had occurred only in the past two months). From there, she pulled the patient surveys for the previous four months and examined every form that rated comfort as average or below. She discovered that in the two months prior to the drop, low comfort scores cited a wide range of issues with low frequency. Starting two months ago, 50 percent of the low comfort scores mentioned coldness and/or the lack of a blanket. Now Poncha had a lead.

Notice that she still didn't know the actual problem. What she had discovered was a symptom: Patients weren't receiving blankets. She had to ask "Why?" again in order to figure out that Frank wasn't supplying them the way he used to. Poncha had to ask "Why?" one more time to determine that Don had given Frank competing priorities. Only at that point did Poncha find the real problem.

NOT EVERY PROBLEM NEEDS A SOLUTION

Now that you've identified the problem, resist the urge to immediately jump in with solutions. After some quick analysis, you may not need to spend any more time on it at all.

• • •

Frustrated at his staff's lack of attention to detail, Marco muttered, "Don't they understand that we don't have any margin of error on this?" He worked extraordinarily long hours trying to control every detail and compensate for the perceived inadequacies of his people. His staff described him as a "powder keg ready to blow." Marco didn't run a nuclear reactor—he ran an agency that supplied food and social support to people in need.

Even if he had run a nuclear power plant, his perception that "we don't have any margin of error" was overstated. Reactors, space ships, and even your favorite mobile phone all have margins of error. There are acceptable operating parameters in everything we do.

Once you clearly identify the problem, ask, "Does this problem need to be solved?" Sometimes the answer is no. For example, when Poncha took the issue to Don, he might have decided that the revenue lost from cold patients was more than offset by increased revenue tied to other changes in the inventory management system (in which case Poncha would have a different problem to discuss: tying nurse evaluations to satisfaction measures on factors outside of their control). Not every problem requires an intervention or solution. These questions can help you decide whether to take action:

1. How likely is this problem to occur in the future?

Was this a freak unlikely event that no amount of planning could have changed, or could it happen again? If you had to put a percentage chance on the probability that the problem would happen again in the next week, quarter, or year, what is that probability?

2. What is the magnitude of the damage if the problem does recur?

Start with qualitative measures. If the problem happens again, what is the impact on your group or the organization: negligible, not good, bad, very bad, or disastrous? Try to quantify the label you used. For example, explain what "bad" means in terms of your metrics (money, time, people, customer impact, etc.).

Once you know the likelihood that the problem will recur and the magnitude of the impact when it does, multiply the two. For instance, Poncha had determined that the problem was 100 percent likely to continue and that the impact was bad, to the tune of 5 to 10 percent lost revenue over the next six months. The math she shared with Don was:

Impact =
1.00 (chance of recurrence) × .075 (5 to 10% revenue loss)
× $100 million (revenue)

In this case the impact, a loss of $7.5 million over six months, was significant, and Don decided to address the issue.

Let's look at a different scenario where the chance the problem will happen again is small (5 percent) and the impact is not good (perhaps five days lost on a six-month project). Now the math looks like this:

Impact =
.05 (chance of recurrence) × .038 (5 days/130 work days in six months)
× $5 million (weekly cost of the project)

In general, the impact of this problem is about $9,500. With a $140 million project budget, that's a problem that is probably not worth spending time on. It's unlikely to happen again and doesn't have massive impact if it does.

3. Is it best to prevent the problem or to mitigate the impact of the problem?

Finally, question whether it's a better use of resources to fix the problem or to mitigate the consequences of the problem. In Poncha's example, mitigating the impact of the problem wouldn't be effective (for instance, having staff call patients and apologize for the lack of blankets). It made more sense to solve the problem and reassign priorities to free up Frank for blanket duty.

In a different situation, it may cost less or even be advantageous to mitigate the consequences rather than solve the problem. For instance, when Apple, Inc., released the Apple Watch, supplies were very limited because one of two manufacturers delivered a defective part. Apple chose to use the limited availability to enhance exclusivity and desirability rather than further delay launch.

Once you know the problem, decide whether you need to address it. Managers who win well know that not every problem requires a solution.

DEFINE WHAT SUCCESS LOOKS LIKE

You've taken responsibility, identified the real problem, and determined that it is a problem you should solve. At this point most managers will generate solutions, but that's premature. Pleasers are anxious to generate a solution—any solution—to get the concerned party off their back, while Users get impatient that there's a problem in the first place. Don't let either source of anxiety keep you from the next tip: Define what success looks like. Establish success criteria so you know when you've successfully resolved the problem.

Establish success criteria so you know when you've successfully resolved the problem. You can't evaluate options until you've clearly defined what a successful solution will accomplish.

In Poncha's situation, she defined success as, "Patient comfort scores return to previous levels without adding significantly to nurse workload or adversely affecting patent care." She was clear about what success looked like when she went to discuss options with Frank and Don. You won't be able to evaluate options until you've clearly defined what a successful solution will accomplish. Here are a few more examples:

- Efficiency improves by 15 percent, doesn't increase costs more than 3 percent, and we've tested and implemented the new process by the end of the quarter.

- Within 24 hours after completion of the job, 100 percent of customers know the outcome of the work we performed for them.

- Every employee has access to current company financials

within 48 hours of their completion and no later than the 15th of the month.

BE CLEAR HOW THE DECISION WILL BE MADE

As with every decision (see Chapter 7), be clear about who owns the decision and how the decision will be made. Before you generate and discuss potential solutions, be clear whether you will be the one to choose or if the group will vote or reach consensus.

GENERATE SOLUTIONS

Now it's time to come up with ideas. When we ask a normal room of managers how they generate solutions, the majority say, "Brainstorming." We invite you to set aside traditional brainstorming. It doesn't work very well for a couple of reasons. First, despite the rule not to judge ideas, everyone does anyway. It's human nature—and it's not a bad thing, because you do want people thinking about how the ideas might fulfill the solution criteria. The second problem with traditional brainstorming is that it doesn't give equal weight to ideas. In most groups, ideas that are shared by people in authority or by persuasive extroverts often gain steam before other ideas that may be as good or better.

To solve these challenges, try some alternatives. One technique we like is to give everyone note cards and ask them to write one to three possible solutions on a card. When everyone has done that, shuffle the cards, redistribute them, and have them read through the ideas on the card they received. Everyone now writes one or more solutions on the card they received. Shuffle and distribute once more, have everyone add an idea, then go around the group and have each person read the ideas on his or her card. Collect the ideas on a whiteboard or flip chart, using hash marks when an idea is repeated. Now every idea is on the board without the weight of a specific person behind it.

COMPARE SOLUTIONS WITH YOUR SUCCESS CRITERIA

As a team, rate the ideas you generated in terms of how well they satisfy the success criteria. Where it's unclear, ask people to advocate for and against the ideas.

CHOOSE A SOLUTION

Unless one clear choice emerged, you've narrowed the list to a few strong candidates, and now you will use the decision-making process you shared at the opening of the discussion.

IMPLEMENT WITH THE WINNING WELL MEETING FORMULA

As with any meeting, this discussion will result in a commitment. Use the Winning Well Meeting Formula so everyone is clear who will do what, by when, and how they will know it's been done. Also, set a specific time when you will evaluate what happened.

EVALUATE THE SOLUTION AND PLAN FOR NEXT TIME

At the agreed-on time, meet with the relevant people and look at real data. How well has your solution worked? Did it do what you intended? What can you learn from this process? Is there something you need to incorporate into future decision making or operating procedures to prevent similar problems?

One final note about problem solving: You'll notice that we did not suggest you go looking for "guilty parties" or people to blame. Users and Pleasers play the blame game, either to motivate performance or to deflect their own responsibility, respectively. Managers who win well, however, avoid the temptation to blame people for problems. When there is a breakdown in personal accountability, they address that directly (see Chapter 7). Otherwise, they focus on solutions and ask "What will you (or we) do differently next time?"

YOUR WINNING WELL ACTION PLAN

Consider a problem you currently face or recently dealt with and ask:

1. How can you (or would you next time) take responsibility for resolving the problem?

2. What is (or was) the real problem?

3. How likely it is to happen again and what would be the magnitude of the impact if it does? Based on the probability of recurrence times the magnitude of impact, is this a problem you should (or would) spend time to resolve?

4. What would success look like when this problem is fully addressed?

5. Are you clear about the success criteria or what success looks like?

6. How was the solution chosen/decision made (or how will it be done)?

For solutions you've already implemented:

1. Were you clear on who would do what by when and how you would know?

2. Did you evaluate the solution and what you can learn from it going forward?

NOTES

1. Charles Kepner and Benjamin Tregoe, *The Rational Manager: A Systematic Approach to Problem Solving and Decision Making* (Princeton, NJ: Kepner–Tregoe, 1976), 57.

CHAPTER 9

How to Delegate So Nothing Falls Through the Cracks

"One should aim not at being possible to understand, but at being impossible to misunderstand."

—QUINTILIAN

You already know you should delegate—who really wants to do everything without help? We trust that you're not so vain as to think you know everything and can do everything better than the people you work with. But if you're like most managers, delegating is a struggle. Do any of these reasons why managers struggle to delegate resonate with you?

- Your people might not do the task as well as you would.

- You have control issues.

- You get frustrated when things aren't done right or well.

- People don't follow through, and you waste more time chasing after unfinished tasks than if you'd just done them yourself.

In our work with managers, we consistently see three delegation mistakes that lead to countless hours of lost time, frazzled
nerves, and frustrated leaders:

1. You delegate process, not outcome.

2. You don't define the finish line.

3. You don't hold people accountable.

If you make these mistakes, you're not alone: We've both done
them all more than once. When you address these mistakes, your
people grow, your team gets more done, and you have more time for
the work only you can do.

• • •

Karin worked with a social media customer service representative
who told her:

"The other day, a customer tweeted at me, 'Are you a bot?' At
first I was really offended and wanted to tweet back 'I AM NOT A
BOT!' But when I thought about it some more, I was sad. I realized
that by following the scripts and all the rules, I sounded very robotic.
That's not what our customers want or need. They come to social
media because they want some upbeat and friendly interaction. I
could provide better service if we had a bit more freedom to do what
we know is right."

It's not just social media reps who feel this way. It happens
across industries at all levels. We've met vice presidents whose fear
has caused a dangerous botlike trance. Bots leading bots is no way to
win well. Sadly, it starts with good intentions: an effort to get everyone on the same page; a PR team that wants to ensure that all
employees share the same story; or efficiency studies that show the
"right way" to do things saves much more time.

We've both heard well-meaning managers say, "I want to take all
the thinking out of it, make it as simple as possible so those employees can just execute efficiently."

While the intention may be good, when you delegate process,
people begin to subtly lose their passion for their work and find
meaning elsewhere.

You may be wondering how you'll know if your employees feel like bots.

Well, first, they stop asking important questions. The "Why?" "What's next?" and, "What if?" questions disappear, but paradoxically, they won't make a move without asking for approval. They need approval for everything, even if it means keeping a customer waiting. What's particularly frustrating is that most of the time your answer is, "Of course."

Another sign is that they "follow the rules" even when the rules don't make sense. Of course the call-center employee should have made an exception for the customer whose spouse had just died, but the guidebook didn't say to, so he stuck to the rules. It's impossible to predict and script every scenario. If an employee can't function outside the playbook, check for bot-building policies.

Finally, if your meetings look like a scene from an old zombie movie and the shuffling dead refuse to talk, or you feel like a cheerleader in an empty stadium, it's likely you've got some folks who've given up the thinking and have slipped into a robotic trance.

So how do you avoid the bot syndrome? Delegate outcomes and be clear on what success looks like, then let your employees work on the best process.

Here are a few examples:

- We need a new product prototype that meets these engineering specifications. . . .

- The task is to come up with a solution to the problem where we do both x and y.

- Your team needs to be trained on the process so they can complete it accurately within ten minutes each month.

When you delegate, be clear about the outcome. What is it they are responsible for achieving? Why is the task meaningful? You may want to specify how this responsibility fits into the bigger picture. Be clear about what a successful outcome looks like, feels like, smells like, what it does—anything that is relevant to the task.

However, do not delegate the process. That is, if the person knows how to do the job you've delegated, resist the urge to tell her how to do it. When you tell a competent person how to do something she already knows how to do, it's insulting and demeaning, and it degrades trust.

When you tell a competent person how to do something she already knows how to do, it's insulting and demeaning, and it degrades trust.

Be clear about the outcome and leave the process to the employee. When you walk someone through the process, that's not true delegation. If he knows how to do the work, you're micromanaging.

We've never met a manager who admits to being a micromanager, but it's a frequent complaint we hear from employees and managers at every level. Micromanaging is a dysfunctional behavior that most leaders fall into from time to time. So how do you know if you're slipping into the micromanagement trap?

It's easy to spot micromanagement when you're the one being micromanaged, but it can be more difficult when you're the culprit. Here are a few examples of micromanagement:

- Constantly telling people what to do and how to do it

- Hypermonitoring even your best employees

- Obsessing about irrelevant details

- Frequently emailing, calling, or otherwise checking on your people while you're on vacation

- Demanding constant reports, feedback, and updates

- Getting nothing done because your employees are waiting for you to do all the work they should be doing

Avoid these symptoms by establishing clear expectations and then delegate the outcome. If the employee never learned how to do the work, she needs training. If you want to train someone to do something, be clear that's what you are doing. Otherwise, delegate outcomes, not process.

DID YOU FAIL TO DEFINE THE FINISH LINE?

Recently, David asked his business manager to complete a specific task. He was clear about the outcome. He thought this task would take two to three days to complete, even with interruptions. He was right in the amount of time he estimated, but when they talked a week later, she had not yet started, much less completed, the project. David was frustrated. He'd been clear about what needed to be done. What was the problem?

The problem was that he'd committed delegation mistake number 2: He never defined the finish line. This is a very common mistake that many managers make, especially Type A driven folks. They delegate a task and mentally expect it to be completed instantly if not sooner, but they don't give their people an actual due date. Then they get frustrated that it's not completed according to their mental calendar. David failed to define the deadline and was frustrated when his unspoken expectation wasn't met.

His business manager said it well: "I can't meet expectations I don't know you have."

Let's be clear here: This is not a problem with your people. David's business manager was working hard on other tasks. She had put the project on her long list of things to be done. Without a defined finish line, she would probably have completed it in two or three weeks as her other work allowed her to get to it. There's nothing wrong with that.

Occasionally we will run into a manager who challenges us on this point. One gentleman explained how he interprets similar situations: "Look, if they had time to do those other things, they had time to do what I asked."

Our response: "That's true, they did have the time. Now, why should they have prioritized your assignment above the other tasks on their list?"

"Because *it was me* who asked for it," he thundered.

We applaud this manager for his honesty. He certainly said what many managers privately think: "If *I* asked for it, it should automatically be a top priority." This is hubris at best and narcissism at worst. Here's a quick reality check that will help you manage effectively and keep your soul intact:

You are not the center of anyone else's world (unless you have a dog—and they fake it pretty well).

To avoid delegation mistake number 2, be clear about the finish line. When does the project need to be completed? For soul-filled leadership, verify that the person can complete the work within that time frame. If there are competing priorities, you might help the employee clarify what is most important or talk about those priorities with the managers who assigned them.

DID YOU BUILD ACCOUNTABILITY INTO THE ASSIGNMENT?

One time when we shared these delegation principles, an audience member stopped us after number 2 and said, "Okay, so I need to be clear about the outcome and when it's due. I think I'm good about that, but things still don't get done. Tell me there's more."

Can you identify with this frustrated manager? How many hours, days, or weeks do you waste chasing down delegated assignments that never come back to you? Have you ever delegated something and been clear about the expected outcome and the finish line only to find yourself wondering six weeks later whatever happened to the project?

We've all been there. Now you're frustrated, upset with the employee, and have to carve out more time to figure out what's happened, and everything is behind schedule. You don't have time for that.

In fact, when you fix this third delegation mistake—failing to build in accountability— you will never again have to chase down a lost assignment. This is the killer mistake, the one that makes so many leaders give up on delegation or else do it with ulcer-causing frustration. When you have to chase after assignments, the missing ingredient is accountability. Effective managers build accountability into the assignment; they don't leave it to chance.

To build accountability into the assignment, schedule a mutual appointment where you will receive the assignment back from the other person. For example:

"This is due June 30. Let's meet for 15 minutes at 3:00 p.m. on June 30. The agenda for the meeting is for you to share the final product/findings/outcome, and we'll discuss follow-up and questions."

Both of you schedule the meeting on your respective calendars. The principle is that when you delegate, there comes a scheduled time where the other person completes the assignment and returns it to you. That's built-in accountability.

If the project is a long one, you might schedule a status update one-third of the way through where the employee is responsible for discussing his approach and early obstacles, and you mutually clarify expectations.

Don't leave accountability to chance. No matter how responsible your people might be, if you don't clearly define how the task or project will be returned to you, other work can get in the way. You might even be the one to assign something else, or they might face competing priorities from another manager.

Schedule a time when you look each other in the eye, and your days of chasing missed deadlines are over.

Remember, delegation is a powerful tool to get more done and help your people grow, but only when you delegate outcomes, clearly define what success looks like, define the finish line, and schedule a follow-up session.

YOUR WINNING WELL ACTION PLAN

1. Think about the next project or task you need to delegate. Take a moment to write down:

   a. What does success look like? What is the expected outcome?

    b. What is your ideal finish line for this task?

    c. When will you schedule a meeting with the employee to receive the project?

2. Think of a task that has recently been delegated to you. Can you list:

    a. What does success look like? What is the expected outcome?

    b. What is your ideal finish line for this task?

    c. When will you return the project?

    d. If you could not answer one or more of these questions, when can you go back to the person who delegated the task and get clarity?

3. Break the micromanagement morass. If you are particularly prone to micromanaging, consider these steps to free yourself (and reclaim your soul):

    a. Consider your motives. What is causing you to micromanage? Get a mentor or coach to help you get to the root cause. Ask for feedback from your team.

    b. Get the right team. If you just can't trust this team, but you have trusted teams in the past, it may be time to take a look at your players.

    c. Set clear expectations. Establishing clear direction up front is the first step to empowering your team. Tell your team where you need them to go, but not how to get there.

    d. Develop a robust communication system. Consider what information you really need to receive and at what frequency. Develop a cadence that make updates easy. You may not be able to go cold turkey, but try to minimize unnecessary reporting.

    e. Give clear feedback. The worst kind of micromanaging is recycling feedback. If something isn't right, be very clear about what you need to avoid endless rework and wasted time.

CHAPTER 10

Get More Done in Less Time

"Simplicity boils down to two steps: Identify the essential. Eliminate the rest."

—LEO BABAUTA

When you care about winning, it's easy to feel overwhelmed. There's always more that you feel you should do, and there never seems to be time to get to all the tasks that matter. Winning Well managers recognize they can't do it all and have a system to identify what matters most and know what to let go.

• • •

"David, I just don't have time. There is so much to do that some days I just want to give up!" Halisee was a midlevel manager in a large software company. She'd sought out coaching because the demands of her job were nearly unbearable. Between the needs of her team members and her supervisor's expectations, she'd been working 60-hour weeks, and her health had deteriorated. She was not winning, and Winning Well seemed out of reach. She hated looking at her calendar with its wall-to-wall meetings, often with two or three appointments competing for the same window of time.

Perhaps you can empathize. Managers face an unending stream of information, problems to solve, decisions to make, fires to put out, interruptions from email, texts, phone calls, messaging apps—and that's not to mention the projects they want to work on to build a better future. At times it can seem like you'll never get ahead. Managers who win well focus their time and energy on the activities that produce results and build relationships.

ACKNOWLEDGE YOU CAN'T DO EVERYTHING

First, you must acknowledge that you cannot do everything. We talk with leaders all the time who are overwhelmed because they haven't come to terms with this reality. We call this Winning Well approach to time "infinite need, finite me." At any moment in time there are literally thousands of things you could be doing, but you get to do only one. That's it. One.

Before you can focus your time and energy for results, you have to reach an understanding with yourself that you can do only one thing at any given moment. It's foolish to believe you really make a difference on that muted conference call while you also try to help the employee who's come in for a quick piece of advice. You're not giving either situation the attention it needs. If the conference call isn't productive, see Chapter 5. If the employee is coming to you with a problem she should be solving herself, see Chapter 14. If both are vital, do them separately.

After that, make peace with the fact that the work never ends. You know this intellectually, but when you truly internalize and make peace with the fact that there's always another thing you could do but won't, you will experience the freedom to focus on what is most important right now.

Infinite need, finite me.

KNOW WHAT MATTERS MOST
IN YOUR ORGANIZATION

Once you've made peace with the reality of infinite need, finite me, it's time to get crystal clear about WMM: what matters most. In your work, what are the two or three most important organizational values, and what are the most important outcomes that move your relationships and results forward? You may put together a long list, but do the work to trim it down to the two or three most critical values and activities. What really drives success for you and your team? You need this clarity in order to take the next steps.

IDENTIFY YOUR
MOST IMPORTANT ACTIVITY

Once you know the values and outcomes that matter most to your organization and the success of your group, you're ready to organize your day around your MIT—the most important thing. Your MIT is the single most important task you can do that day.

At the start of each day, look over your projects, tasks, and to-dos and select the one item that is the MIT for that day. Hint: It should align with your WMM values and activities. Your MIT will often change from day to day. Be clear about that one thing. Now you're ready for the next step.

DO IT

Do your MIT first.

You will be distracted. Real issues will come up, you'll face a change of direction, your boss will need something—life happens. Be clear about your MIT and do it first—before email, before voice mail, before checking in with your boss or your team. Whether it takes 30, 60, or 90 minutes, you'll be done and ready to deal with everything else.

Think about a normal work year. If you work 50 weeks each year, that's 250 work days, minus a few holidays. That makes 250 MITs. What would happen to your people, your results, and your career if you seriously accomplished 250 MITs each year? Most managers are shocked at what they can achieve.

And remember: While you're focused on your MIT, be sure that your employees know theirs and that you are not the one to interrupt them or keep them from it.

RULE OF ONE

Focus your time and energy with the Rule of One. We mentioned earlier that you can do only one thing at a time. When you work on your MIT, turn off your phone, your email, your Facebook and Twitter notifications (unless like in some social media companies, your MIT really is to check Twitter), and focus on that MIT.

Brooke was vice president for a global education nonprofit. She chose to implement the Rule of One by designating 90 minutes in the morning and 90 minutes in the afternoon as "head down" time that could only be interrupted for true emergencies. She created the time so that she could focus on her daily MITs, but she discovered that the entire office's productivity improved because everyone else did the same thing.

If you spend time with successful C-level executives, you'll see that they do not multitask. They focus. They're all in. Concentrating. They're confident that their focus will make an impact. They're humble enough to realize that their brain won't offer great insights in scattered directions at the same time.

There's almost nothing in life that can't wait 90 minutes, and if it can't wait, someone will come find you. The Rule of One means that you give one thing at a time your full attention. When you need to change focus, do so intentionally and fully.

REST

Your brain and body function better with rest. This is why "infinite need, finite me" is the foundation to getting more done in less time. We've worked with countless User managers who haven't come to terms with their own limitations. They run themselves ragged with little sleep and no vacation, and they don't invest time in important personal relationships. Busy doesn't mean productive. Be intentional with time to restore your productivity.

If this is difficult for you, we understand. David hates having to sleep. The world is so interesting and full of amazing things to learn and do that for many years he operated on five hours of sleep every night. But he paid a price. He got sick, gained weight, was irritable, and had less energy to make decisions. People vary, but most adults thrive with seven to eight hours of sleep. What do you need to renew your mind and physical health? If you are constantly tired and run down and can't focus or hold an idea in your head for very long, do yourself and your people a favor: rest. You'll get more done.

EXERCISE

Most managers we've worked with say they're "too busy to exercise." They just don't know how they can fit it into their packed schedules.

It's a paradox, but when you carve out time to exercise, that energy and time is returned to you many times over. Your thinking is clearer, your physical energy increases, you sleep better, and stress doesn't bother you as much. Do walking meetings rather than sitting in a conference room. Exercise during your favorite TV show. Get your heart rate up every day and you'll get more done in less time.

WORK WITH PURPOSE

Know your "Why?" Why are you doing what you're doing? This is the answer to many questions, especially when you don't feel like doing it, and it genuinely takes real effort to manage. What is your purpose? Why did you take this role?

There are five reasons managers usually take their jobs. The five "Ps" of management motivation are:

Power

Prestige

Purse or Pennies

Purpose

People

When you work from the first three motivations, you often run out of steam because there's never enough power, fame, or money for your sacrifice and work. When you lack motivation, come back to your big "Why?"—the people and purpose in your work. Let it ground you and motivate you.

KNOW YOURSELF

What gives you energy and what depletes it?

David is an introvert. He loves to be with people, but he also knows that extended time with people depletes his energy. If he goes too long without solitude, it can actually make him sick. When he conducts multiday workshops, he will often explain that he wants to be his best for the workshop and will forgo one night of fun with the participants in order to recharge his batteries. Karin's an extrovert. She loves ideas and action. She shows up better after a night-of-fun energy exchange. When she spends too much time writing nonstop or on organizational details, it drains her. She can do it, but she is deliberate about when and how much, and she may need a nap.

Know your daily energy patterns and schedule activities that suit your energy. When do you do your best thinking? For many people, it's in the morning while their brain and body are fresh. If you have an afternoon dip, can you use that time to do routine tasks that don't require as much energy?

MAKE FEWER DECISIONS

You use energy to make decisions. The more decisions you make in a day, the more difficult it becomes to make the next one. Stop making decisions you don't need to make.

- Insist that people on your team make decisions they should make.

- Unsubscribe from unhelpful email that saps your decision-making energy.

- Make low-risk decisions quickly. If the consequences are minimal, make decisions quickly and move on.

- Make decisions once. This is an old and essential productivity tool. Look at an email once, then either delete it, act on it, schedule it for future action, put it in a file related to its project, or put it in a "maybe read later" file.

NO MORE LOOSE ENDS

The final way to ensure that you get more done in less time is to ruthlessly deal with any activities that sap your time. We've given you tools to address the biggest culprits: meetings, decisions, problems, and delegation. End every meeting with the Winning Well Meeting Formula: Who does what, by when, and how will you know? Bring clarity and accountability to every meeting, every decision, and every delegated task so you don't have to waste an ounce of energy chasing after unfinished work. Be consistent with your accountability. These little investments of time add up to weeks, if not months, of found time. They also free your mind from worry and anxiety, which in turn allows you to better focus on the task at hand.

YOUR WINNING WELL ACTION PLAN

1. Embrace "infinite need, finite me." Identify one or two specific activities you could stop doing to free up time for more important work.

2. Look at your next three days. Right now, identify your MIT for each of those days. Write them down.

3. At the end of each of the next three days, give yourself a grade "A" to "F" on how well you spent your time on the MIT.

4. Take a piece of paper and make two columns. On the left side list all the things that make you feel more energetic and alive. On the right side list the things that deplete your energy. Now make a specific plan for how you can do more of at least two items in column one, and less of at least two items in column two.

5. Do you get the rest and exercise you need to be at your best on most days? If not, what is one change you can make to help yourself in this area?

6. Where do you need to be intentional about clarity and accountability with meetings, decisions, problems, and delegation? Are there any other frequent energy drains you need to address?

CHAPTER 11

How and Why to Terminate Employees with Grace and Dignity

"To part is the lot of all mankind."
—R. M. BALLANTYNE

Now, you might think Winning Well managers have everyone focused on the right behaviors, hold them accountable, and inspire greatness, so there would be no need to fire anyone. Sadly, even the strongest managers find themselves in situations where the best solution for all parties is to part ways. Winning Well managers know how to fire someone with grace and dignity.

• • •

"My name is Mary. Can I talk with you a minute?"

David had just finished delivering a leadership skills program for a gathering of middle-level managers and executives. Mary had come up afterward to introduce herself and share her experience.

"I was the vice president of a well-known technology company, and I consistently did everything you just talked about—with one exception. I let people stay who weren't right for the team."

David replied, "You're not alone. That's a difficult challenge for most managers."

Mary frowned. "Yes it is. It's also why I said 'I *was* the vice president.' I lost my job because I didn't practice adequate accountability. Please make sure people know how important this is. Tell them Mary said so."

Well, Mary—this is for you:

Recently, the human resources firm TINYhr conducted a survey that asked, "What would you do if you got to be boss for a day?"

How might you answer this question? How do you think your employees would answer it?

We first saw this survey 20 years ago, and, curiously, the number one answer had not changed. The number one answer wasn't give myself a raise, take more vacation, or put better food in the break room. More respondents said they would "fire, demote, or make other changes to improve employee caliber" than anything else.[1]

Now, we've both been around long enough to know that some of the people choosing this as their number one response might lack self-awareness and actually be at the top of your removal list. Nevertheless, with its consistent results across decades, the survey underscores the need for you to practice accountability.

Managers often have to fire people, but there is a huge difference between managers who do it well and those who make it a terrible, humiliating experience. Firing someone is one of the most difficult things most managers ever have to do. Even so, removing a person from your team or work group is an important part of winning. Removing poor performers tells your contributing people that you value their time and effort. When you remove troublesome individuals, you help everyone be more productive—especially you. In our experience, a troublesome poor performer can soak up 80 percent of your time when you don't take proper care of the situation.

So yes, if you're going to win, there will come a time when you need to fire people. How you do it determines if you win well. This trips up many managers.

For example, it may feel easy to fire someone you've never cared for, who treated you and everyone else rudely and abused customers, but what about when you really like the person? You've grown close over the years. You care about her. You might even know her family. Perhaps she's even a strong performer who did something stupid. Now you have to fire her. How do you do that?

Before anything else, let's start with a strong caveat: We are not employment-law attorneys. You absolutely need to talk with your human resource folks, or, if you're in a smaller organization and don't have that avenue available, talk with an attorney or your local employers council. It's your responsibility to be clear about the institution's rules, contracts (e.g., vis-à-vis unions or tenure), and any federal and state laws affecting your situation. That's not what we want to address. Rather, we hope to help you with mindsets and practices that will help you terminate employees with grace and dignity when it is the best course of action.

HOW TO GET OKAY WITH A TOUGH DECISION

Many managers struggle with the decision to remove an employee from the team. This isn't a bad thing—you should take it seriously. David once worked alongside the owner of a large construction firm. When they spoke about firing employees, the owner said, "If you ever reach a place where you can affect a person's livelihood and family without a second thought, then it's time for *you* to resign."

You should take it seriously and give it that second thought but be aware of the temptation to put it off or avoid it. Terminating employment can be a very emotional decision. That's why so many managers avoid it. You might feel like you don't want to hurt the person or his family. If you're a Pleaser Manager, you want people to like you. Even Users can procrastinate on these decisions. In order to move past this paralysis, you'll need to change your mindset.

When you manage, there will come a time when you realize a person is no longer committed to the mission and is not, or never was, a good fit for the organization. In these situations, you want to be sure you've made reasonable efforts to help her (reinforce expectations, alert her to the issue, provide any needed training, and practice your company's due process if it has one). If you've done this and it's clear that the person needs to move on, the most important thing you can do for your team, for your own credibility, and for the employee is to help her go.

You should weigh the issues and make thoughtful decisions, but there will still be times when asking an employee to leave is necessary. Don't do it because other people think you should, don't do it because you're angry, and don't do it to avoid other problems. When you terminate, do it because it is best for the team, the organization, and that employee.

Not Everyone Belongs Here

One fundamental mindset to embrace before you can help your people achieve results together is that not everyone is meant to be a part of every group, team, or organization.

On the surface this may seem self-evident, and yet you've probably been a part of an organization or team that suffered because those with the responsibility to ensure fit and mission alignment did not do their job. At the heart of terminating employees with grace and dignity is the understanding that the human being in front of you has strengths and value—strengths and value that just don't work for his current position.

Karin worked with an HR manager who had lots of big ideas but constantly suffered in execution. After a year of reviewing expectations, performance-improvement planning, training, and straight talk, she had to let him go. A year later he called her and said:

"Thank you. Getting fired was one of the best things that ever happened to me. I'm working on my Ph.D., teaching, and consulting. In hindsight, I should have quit, but I was too scared about what to do next. This forced me into needed action."

If you need to fire someone, it doesn't really matter if she did something wrong or simply isn't an ideal fit. We're talking about a mindset that you bring to the process: This isn't personal, and not everyone is meant to be a part of every team.

You Serve Them Too

One of the most important pieces of the termination decision is the awareness that when you help someone move on, you serve that person too. This is a vital part of knowing how to say good-bye: realizing that you don't do an employee any favors by tolerating poor performance, mission misalignment, or abuse of coworkers.

When you help someone move on, you serve that person too. You don't do an employee any favors by tolerating poor performance, mission misalignment, or abuse of coworkers.

In the case of mission misalignment, if you don't say good-bye, you keep the person from learning more about his strengths. In the instance where you tolerate negligence or abuse, you enable poor behavior and prevent the individual from learning how to succeed in the real world.

In either case, while saying good-bye to employees is not pleasant or something you would look forward to, it can definitely be an act of caring if your motivations center both on what is best for the individual and on what is best for the organization.

Don't allow your lack of courage or your discomfort to hurt your poor performers and your good ones. Great managers know when and how to say good-bye because they recognize that in doing so they express value for their team, for the mission, and even for the departing staff member.

HOW DO I DO THIS?

First, do your homework. When you prepare properly, you make it less likely you'll run into problems with termination decisions.

That's why we stress the importance of clear expectations. If you get frustrated with an employee's performance but your expectations weren't clear, that's your fault, not hers. Be diligent with clear expectations, know your company's policies and procedures, and go through the right processes to help the person perform or prepare for termination.

Now let's assume you've done all the work leading up to the termination decision. You've clarified expectations, provided necessary training, followed your company's policies, given appropriate second chances, and still, it did not work out. Now you are stuck with "How?" Once again, when we say "How?" we are not providing legal advice; we want to help you go through the process in a way that maintains your dignity and the employee's.

Human resource professionals will rightly tell you to keep the conversation short, clear, and direct. Generally, in the presence of a witness, you will tell the employee what is happening, have her pack, and escort her off-site. Don't apologize. Be aware of security issues; we've both conducted terminations where we had extra security planted around the corner in case things got "crazy" with an employee who had been abusive or threatening.

WHEN YOU WANT TO SAY MORE

Terminating someone's employment can be difficult, but it's important that you keep your composure. One time, David had an HR representative along as a witness, and the rep actually got misty-eyed and nearly started crying, sympathizing with the employee who had lost his job. That's not professional, it makes a difficult situation very awkward, and it can even create legal problems down the road. When your heart calls for more than a simple, straightforward statement, keep in mind:

1. This is not about you.

It can be tempting to express your own difficulty or emotional anguish when you have to let someone go.

Don't.

A simple, neutrally worded statement along the lines of, "These conversations are not easy" is adequate. Anything more dramatic or emotional than that makes the conversation about you and not about the other person. Whatever emotional stresses you might experience in the situation pales compared to the employee's. She just lost her job. Keep your focus on serving her by being clear, concise, and supportive.

2. He *did* something wrong; he *isn't* something wrong.

Be clear about the behavior or reason for termination. Reference "these actions" and not the person. For example, "These unexcused absences have resulted in . . ." as opposed to "You're undependable." This mistake does not define the person. Give him a chance to talk if he needs a minute.

3. She has a future and could use some hope.

Help her to fail forward. Karin tries to plant a seed about an optimistic future, even if she's furious with what the employee has done. For example, she might say, "You don't have to let this define you. I've seen many people who've bounced back from what appeared devastating at the time to have vibrant careers."

4. Allow space for questions.

It is compassionate to say something like, "I know this can be a lot to take in. Do you have any questions about the process or what needs to happen next?" (Note that you did not open the door to questions about the decision. If he questions or challenges the decision, return to a gently worded, "I know this can be difficult. This will be your last day, and we will . . .," then redescribe the process.) Be sure he knows whom to contact in the event he has questions about any loose ends.

5. You can say good-bye.

We've never regretted taking a moment to connect and say good-bye. If you were close, it's okay to say something personal if it feels right. David has had to fire several people who remained friends afterward even though they weren't the right fit for the position.

Compassionate leaders stay compassionate. Stay firm, don't backpedal, but it's okay to connect and say, "Good-bye," and, "You can survive this."

YOUR WINNING WELL ACTION PLAN

1. If you've ever fired someone, recall that experience. Based on what we've discussed here, what, if anything, would you do differently the next time?

2. What beliefs about firing people keep you from doing it or doing it well with grace and dignity? What alternate beliefs might you consider?

3. Have you ever been fired? If so, what happened in the experience that you would want to duplicate for others? How would you improve the experience?

4. Are your expectations as clear as you think they are? (Avoid frustrating and unnecessary terminations by regularly checking for understanding, asking employees what they're doing and why they're doing it.)

5. If you haven't done so recently, pay your HR department, attorney, or local employers council a visit and ask to be walked through the most critical laws, policies, or processes that apply to your situation.

NOTES

1. TINYhr, "Employee Wishlists for 2015," accessed February 7, 2015, http://www.tinyhr.com/landing-page/2015-new-year-employee-report.

Winning Well— Motivate, Inspire, and Energize Your Team

In Section 2 you received tools to help you and your people achieve results, stay focused, and prevent assignments from falling through the cracks. These practices are all about winning.

In Section 3 you receive the tools to win well—that is, to sustain excellence and results over time. We'll work from your employees' perspective as we focus on what they need most: to be seen, trusted, supported, connected, included, challenged, and recognized—and to have some fun along the way. We'll share the skills you need to connect with, invest in, and collaborate with your people. Tapping into these deeply human needs is what makes the difference between just winning and Winning Well. Adopt these simple techniques and you'll avoid the soul-sucking slippery slope so many Users, Gamers, and Pleasers find themselves sliding down—along with their long-term results.

CHAPTER 12

The Secret to Releasing Your People's Energy

"Our chief want is someone who will inspire us to be what we know we could be."

—RALPH WALDO EMERSON

Y ou can't motivate your employees. By definition, motivation comes from inside a person. It's not something you can provide externally. If you could, the Gallup Polls wouldn't consistently be showing that 68 to 70 percent of American workers are disengaged (with similar statistics around the world).[1] That's why most employee-engagement programs don't work. You can, however, cultivate motivation by uncovering it, tapping into it, and inspiring lasting change. But you can't just dive into a discussion like that. It begins when you create the space to know your employees for who they truly are.

• • •

Shelly was completely frustrated with her team's results. She'd brought in extra training, introduced a clever incentive program, stack ranked and managed the outliers, implemented every best practice she could find, and even invited her boss in for a quick motivational talk.

Nothing worked. The team's results were still abysmal, and staff showed visible signs of exhaustion.

"What can you tell me about the people you supervise?" her manager, Laura, asked. Shelly's response was filled with "attitude problems," "absence issues," and a smattering of statistics.

Laura tried again. "What can you tell me about the human beings on your team? Are they married? Do they have kids? What do they do for fun? What do they enjoy most on the weekends? What did they do last weekend?"

After a bit of a blank stare, Shelly admitted, "With results like these, I don't have time to ask about all that. Plus, this is business; it's not personal."

"Which team leader is knocking it out of the park?" Laura asked.

"Jose," she said, without hesitation.

"Please go talk to Jose again. But this time, don't ask him about best practices; ask him how he connects with his staff."

Shelly came back with a laundry list of connection builders Jose did on a regular basis and tried them. She met each employee at the door as he came in; spent the first two hours of each day doing nothing but sitting side by side with call-center reps; started each one-on-one talking about something personal; gave birthday cards; and followed up on "no big deal" stuff such as how her kid did in the soccer game last week.

Results soared. Business is always personal.

WALK WITH THEM AND THEY'LL WALK WITH YOU

To a manager, values and vision are important, but they're only half the equation. David learned this in a poignant exchange with a boy named Eric.

When he was 23 years old, David taught a course in community leadership at an urban high school. A major part of the course involved public speaking. On the ninth day of class, Eric, a solidly built 17-year-old junior, stood in the front of the class to deliver his first impromptu speech. Between the scar on his cheek, the tattoos covering his thick arms, and his relaxed confidence, he exuded tough. The other students treated him accordingly.

He reached into a hat, pulled out a slip of paper, and announced his topic. "I got cars, y'all."

Eric shifted his weight from side to side, looked out the window, and avoided eye contact with anyone in the class. Finally, he took a deep breath, shook his head, and began.

"Cars is tight . . . ."

But that was all he could get out. Nerves got the better of Eric, and he slid back into his desk, defeated. After class, David asked Eric to stay behind for a few minutes.

When the other students had left the room, Eric walked up to David and said, "'Sup?"

"Eric, I—"

But the words caught in David's throat.

What's up?

It was a good question.

He'd asked Eric to stay after class so he could offer encouragement, but David was barely six years older than Eric, had led a different life from his, and had been a teacher for less than two weeks.

What was "up" was that David had no clue.

With the empty encouragement lodged in his throat, David scrambled for something to say. Eric had a piece missing from the top of his ear. It may have been shallow, but it was the best David could do.

"Eric, do you mind if I ask you what happened to your ear?"

"Yeah mister. Was a bullet. It ricocheted off a dumpster and got my ear." No bravado. Nonchalant. Like it happened every day.

He pulled up his left pant leg. "Got one in my leg too." He pointed to a scar on his shin. "Doc says they can't take it out."

Then he grinned. "It makes the metal detector go off at the courthouse."

As his story unfolded, Eric explained that he'd been involved in gangs since he was 11. He'd been in several gunfights at age 12. As David and Eric got to know one another, it became clear that Eric was trying to leave behind the gang life. He'd started his own landscaping business, had been beaten out of his gang (which is exactly what it sounds like, only worse), and had chosen classes like the one where he met David.

One day David asked him what had prompted him to change.

"Last year," he said, "here in Denver and out in Cali, I went to 11 different funerals. Some were friends, some were family."

He paused and stared at his shoes.

"After that last one, man I looked up and I was like, 'This ain't normal!' I gotta do something."

Teachers often claim they learn as much or more from their students as they're able to teach. David knows that to be true. From Eric, he learned an invaluable principle: You do not motivate people.

Eric had his own motivations. He was in the course for his own reasons. He had challenges, values, and concerns David knew nothing about. Until David learned what was important to Eric, how to help him achieve what he valued, and how to help him get where he wanted to go, David could not lead him.

As his teacher, David also had his own vision, his own values, his own picture of a future that Eric could not yet see for himself. As a manager, your values and your vision are also important. You shouldn't set them aside. However, if you want people to walk with you, you must first walk with them. Discover what's important to them.

- Why are they a part of the organization?

- What do they value?

- What do they dream of for their future?

When you walk beside them and support them in that purpose, those values, and their dreams, while also sharing your own, then, and only then, you will see true motivation. Walk with them and they'll walk with you.

David had the privilege of being Eric's teacher for two years. He became a leader within the class, succeeded in giving presentations much longer than just 60 seconds, and became a mentor for younger students in the community.

MORE STRATEGIES TO UNLEASH ENERGY

In order to release your people's energy, you must first recognize that you cannot motivate anyone. Motivation always comes from inside your employees. Your job is not to motivate them but to cultivate an environment that releases their internal motivations. Here are three more strategies you can use to unleash your people's motivation.

1. Hold deeper developmental discussions.

When you want to go deeper but you don't want to cross any inappropriate boundaries, there are a number of engaging topics you can use. These topics will open the door and help you learn more about your employees.

You might start with their big dreams. Most development conversations focus on potential next steps, or a five-year plan. What other big dreams do your employees hold in their hearts? What do they want to become? What's on their bucket lists? Is there any way to build some related work or skills into their current jobs? It's motivating to work on your big dream, even in baby steps.

Don't motivate. Cultivate.

From there, you can ask, "What motivates you?" Asking is a good start; however, you can also learn a lot through observation. Pay attention to get insights that will serve as excellent fodder for a deeper dialogue. You can use this as a starter: "You seem really excited about this project. What aspects make it most meaningful for you?" Ask these sorts of questions with sincere curiosity and willingness to hear the answers. You want to build openness and trust, not interrogate your employees or punish them for answers you don't like.

As you deepen your connection with employees, you may be able to ask about what scares them. This one is trickier, and it's not one to start with in new relationships. However, as your relationship develops, getting underneath fear and uncertainty can go a long way in helping someone grow. When you help an employee face her fears and overcome them, it leads to confidence and competence.

One question to incorporate at the beginning of your work relationship and to revisit throughout your time together is, "What do you really need from me?" The power in this question is to keep asking as the relationship matures. You will likely get more real answers as trust increases and the employee grows.

Here's a question that may feel risky, but isn't: "What matters more to you than this job?"

Would we really ask employees this question? Yes—depending on the relationship, maybe not in exactly those words, but the premise is important. What do they care deeply about? Their children? Their place of worship? Their hobbies? Their aging parents? Their health? You want to know what really matters. A little knowledge can go a long way to make you a more supportive manager and bring out much more energy and productivity from your people.

These conversations evolve over time. Don't fire all these questions at your employees in one sitting. Bring them in gently as the relationship grows and you will build trust and know how to support and invest in your people, and you will inspire their best work.

2. Let your employees outgrow their past.

Antoine was an accomplished millennial sales rep in a retail store of a large company who was considered "a bit rough around the edges." He had a "no BS" approach that created a natural bond with entrepreneurs and mom-and-pop companies but left some managers scratching their heads.

Antoine was maxing out his compensation and winning big vacations as rewards for stellar sales year after year, but he wanted more. He went back to college at night and got his degree. He waited until he was selling more to businesses from his store than his counterparts who worked full time in business sales. Then he applied for a job with the business sales manager.

He was rejected. He applied again. Rejected.

His mentor, Jill, encouraged him to shave his scraggly goatee and begin wearing suits to work. He applied again. This time he didn't even get an interview—just a call from HR saying he "wasn't quite ready."

Frustrated, Jill got sneaky. She called up Jack, the hiring manager, and described an ideal candidate she'd like to refer to him. Jill described everything about Antoine without using his name. Jack salivated and asked for the resume as soon as possible. After all, Jack didn't want to risk losing a candidate like that.

Jill sent over Antoine's resume.

Embarrassed, Jack gave Antoine a chance in a junior role, a level down from the position for which Antoine had applied. Within six months he was running circles around his peers, was promoted, and began teaching others his secrets to success.

Most employees mature over time. Even so, when someone has been with a company a long time, it's his old image that sticks. Be sure you're helping your employees outgrow their past.

We've seen too many companies go in search of the ideal candidate, hire her, and then find they had the right person all along. In fact, we've both been that person.

Be brave enough to see who's really showing up.

Anticipate maturity and watch it flourish.

Be an advocate. It's easy to see Antoine as the little Tony he once was: young, overly direct, and a little too cool for the corporate scene.

If you have a company of Jacks you can't win well because you'll squander potential. In this case, Jack didn't see the need to invest in new talent because he was already winning—his numbers were solid. What he couldn't see was the need to think long term and groom raw talent to build a winning future and a reputation of being someone people want to work for.

Are you a Jack or a Jill?

3. Give your employees new challenges.

Meet Larry. Larry's Ph.D. dissertation was on the migratory behavior of striped bass in the Chesapeake Bay, probably not the obvious choice to become chief financial officer of a world-renowned research institution.

But Larry's career was bit like Forest Gump's: He was at the right place at the right time, and then just figured it out. He held many diverse leadership positions between his first assignment in radar-signal processing and his chief financial officer role, including helping to lead a team of engineers building a space telescope.

If you ask Larry about his career path, he cites a series of mentors who took a chance on him and assured him that he would "figure it out."

When you have an employee who's great in his current role, it's sometimes difficult to see him doing anything else, especially something radically different. After all, he's winning, so why rock the boat?

If you want to win well and unlock deep potential for lasting impact for your high performer and your organization, take that quick study and move her into a role that may feel a bit crazy to you and to her. If it doesn't work out, you can recover.

Larry—who, by the way, is Karin's father—ended up helping more than fish, partly because he learned the Winning Well art of taking a chance on talent, as others had done for him. Nothing energizes an employee quite like the feeling that he's just jumped out of an airplane and discovered he has a parachute he didn't even know existed.

Do you have a Larry on your team?

YOUR WINNING WELL ACTION PLAN

1. Write down all your employees' names and what you know about each of them. Here are some options:

   - The name of their significant other
   - What they do for fun
   - Their birthday
   - Talents they are proud of
   - Volunteer work they do
   - What makes them feel most engaged and alive at work

- What makes them crazy at work

- What they see as the next step in their career

If you can't answer these, get to know them more deeply, up to their level of comfort.

2. Meet with all your employees to discuss each one's career. Work to identify three possible stretch projects or assignments that would challenge them to stretch their skills. Agree on next steps and a timeline to pursue at least one of the stretch activities.

NOTE

1. For example, see Nikki Blacksmith and Jim Harter, "Majority of American Workers Not Engaged in Their Jobs," Gallup Poll, October 28, 2011, accessed October 15, 2014, http://www.gallup.com/poll/150383/Majority-American-Workers-Not-Engaged-Jobs.aspx; Daniela Yu and Rajesh Srinivasan, "Employee Engagement Increases in China, but Still Very Low," Gallup Poll, February 20, 2013, accessed November 2014, http://www.gallup.com/poll/160190/employee-engagement-increases-china-low.aspx.

CHAPTER 13

How to Create Confidence and Momentum

"The best way to figure out if you can trust somebody is to trust them."

—ERNEST HEMINGWAY

It isn't what you think or say, it's what you do that communicates trust—or lack of it. The best way to get your team to trust you is to trust them. Trust begets trust. Hire for trust. Require trust. Rid your team of untrustworthy players. Then show your team how much you trust them.

• • •

When John needed something, he wanted it fast, and nothing made him want it faster than when the request was coming from his boss. John, with User reasoning, figured that the most efficient way to get his answer and know that it was right was to text all of his direct reports the question at the same time and ask for the information he needed.

He'd wait for at least two people to respond, and if they had the same answer, he'd send it up the chain.

Each of his employees wanted to please John, so they dropped what they were doing and scrambled to get the answers. Which led all of them to Bob, the data guy, all in the same ten-minute window.

Bob, rightfully irritated, asked, "You do know three other people just asked for that information, right?"

"Err, nope."

It took a few of these fire drills before the managers realized what was going on, and they were ticked.

They asked each other, "Why would he waste our time like that? Doesn't he trust us? Doesn't he value our time?"

After some time spent fuming, they came up with a work-around.

When the text came in, the first one to receive it would go to Bob, and Bob would give everyone the same answer, which they would all forward to John.

After receiving all the responses with identical words, John knew he'd been found out.

Although the managers eventually told John they didn't appreciate the wasted effort, he never fully understood how hurt they were by his apparent need to quadruple verify their work.

Another client we worked with had a similar problem.

Ron, a CEO of a multimillion-dollar organization, put out an order that he had to personally approve all purchases, whether budgeted or not. The staff, particularly the executive team, was frustrated. They had a track record of sound financial management and couldn't understand why the CEO had lost trust in them.

When we spoke with the CEO about the trust issue, it became clear that he was afraid they weren't going to make their revenue numbers. "I trust all of my people. I just have to know what's going on."

Rather than trust the executive staff to solve the problem, he tried to seize control and do everything by himself. He couldn't see the contradiction between the need to have total control and the lack of trust it communicated.

Without John and Ron intending it, their User behaviors had

stunted their employees' confidence and momentum. In both cases it was their behavior that communicated a lack of trust. The sad truth is that both of these managers would have said they trusted their people.

Have you ever worked with a John or Ron? How did they make you feel?

HOW TO SHOW YOUR EMPLOYEES YOU TRUST THEM

It takes more than words to demonstrate your trust in your team. Here are several behaviors that will help you show your employees you trust them.

1. Set audacious goals.

Oh sure, your team may grumble, but managers who win well know there's no greater gift you can give your team than leading them toward head-turning results.

Set the bar high and then tell them, "I believe in you. I know what this team is capable of. Now let's figure out just how, together." Show trust by believing it's possible.

2. Believe in them.

We watched Sam, a manager in a small nonprofit, handle this masterfully with his direct report. The organization worked to ensure water quality in mountain streams. Laura, a free spirit who cared passionately about her people and clean water, managed a team of paid engineers and volunteer inspectors. She worked hard, but her team wasn't satisfied with her performance. They wanted to see her in the field more; she didn't know how she could make them happy, and she didn't feel she was making a big enough impact in a cause she cared deeply about. She came into Sam's office, slumped down in a folding chair, and declared, "I'm done." She said she would turn in her resignation, that she'd lost faith in her ability to be effective.

Sam was devastated. She was one of his rock stars. How had he missed conveying that to her? Sam did not accept her resignation.

"You may have lost your belief in yourself, but you have a problem," he said.

"I do? What's that?"

"I still believe in you. You can quit on yourself, but don't expect me to quit on you."

Of course, that conversation was only the start. It eventually led to Laura's taking a more balanced view of her accomplishments and gaining the confidence she needed to continue her vital work.

Show trust by believing in their capabilities.

3. Invite them to come along.

Early in her career, one of Karin's first bosses, Gail, brought Karin with her to senior-level meetings, arguing that "no one could explain it better" than she could. Of course, that wasn't true; Gail was a seriously gifted explainer. She trusted Karin would do okay and was secure enough to give up the spotlight.

We are amazed at how many bosses are afraid to give such opportunities to their team.

Show trust by sharing the stage.

4. Admit what you don't know.

Show your team you trust them by admitting you don't have all the answers. Trust them with your concerns. You'll be surprised how your people rise to the occasion when you trust them with your questions.

Show trust by being real.

5. Encourage them to meet without you.

A great way to show trust in your team is to give them a big hairy problem and ask them to meet to figure it out. Be sure to define what success looks like. Get any information, criteria, and parameters they may need out of your head and into theirs first—otherwise they'll spin their wheels.

Show trust by getting out of the way.

6. Tell them.

This one might seem obvious, but it works. Can you imagine how good it feels to hear, "I really trust you because . . . "?

Show trust by telling them why.

7. Correct and move on.

If an employee screws up, talk about it, help her learn, and then move on. Show trust by letting it go.

TRUST INSPIRES MOMENTUM

Bill is a retail store director who lived in a trust-but-verify culture. What this meant was that he and every executive above him were expected to constantly show up in stores to experience what was happening, as the customers would.

Is there a bird's nest over the front entrance risking bird poop falling on a customer's head? Are customers being served in a timely way? Did the store look inviting, with all lightbulbs on and everything dusted and ready to go? Were the employees up to speed on the latest products and services? Can the store managers articulate their key initiatives and what they could do to improve?

There was no question: Knowing an exec could stop in at any time kept everyone on their toes. The stores undoubtedly were cleaner and the customer service better as a result.

Of course, these visits were always stressful. The general sentiment was that there was "no such thing as a good visit"—the best you could hope for was "not a bad one."

Which is why Bill came up with an idea to change the experience.

Every summer, instead of the usual pop-in store visits, Bill rented a van, wrapped it in the company logo and fun graphics, and hit the road for a month visiting stores.

The schedule was announced ahead of time, and there was one big rule: Employees would receive only positive feedback, celebration, and fun.

If something was wrong, Bill would quietly call the manager's attention to it or, if it were a small thing like an unplugged sign, he would just plug it in and fix it himself when no one was looking.

These tours had a clear goal: to notice what was right. He did his homework and came prepared with all kinds of recognition, along with a token of appreciation for every employee.

His operations manager came along and took tons of pictures of every visit. Every evening, they created an upbeat collage that included the names of everyone recognized and why. The "postcard" was emailed to the entire region every evening.

The other store directors jokingly referred to the month as Bill's "love tour," but Bill was confident enough to withstand the razzing.

The truth is, the employees loved the love.

Results skyrocketed during that time. The employees wanted to be on top of their game when the tour stopped by their store, and, as you can imagine, there was not a bird's nest in sight. Everything was dusted and ready to go, and the employees knew all about the latest products and services.

These planned visits caused everyone to go through their checklists and remember what a great store experience looked like. This was so much more effective than a "Gotcha" pop-in visit. Yes, Bill still had to show up unannounced at other times. Winning Well requires holding people accountable. But the love tour helped remind employees of what they were capable of doing and gave him an opportunity to say, "Thank you."

Is there someone on your team who could use a little love?

Trust your employees to rise to the occasion, and they will.

Sounds easy, right? But we know a lot of managers who fumble their managing by walking around (MBWA). We encourage you to get out with your people, and as you do, avoid these common traps.

WHY MBWA BECOMES OCHTC ("OH CRAP, HERE THEY COME")

When David's daughter adopted her cat, Twinkie, from the city animal shelter, they took her to the veterinarian for a physical and shots. At the end of the visit, the veterinarian suggested that they put Twinkie in her cat carrier for something other than trips to the vet.

"You don't want her to only associate the cat carrier with the vet. From their perspective, nothing good ever happens to a cat at the vet."

Despite the vet's good advice, David didn't follow through, and Twinkie came to loathe that carrier. When she saw it coming, she'd hiss and run in the other direction.

What do your people do when they see you coming?

Hopefully they don't hiss, but it's possible they run in the other direction. That's what "Oh crap, here they come!" (OCHTC) looks like—they associate you only with something bad.

Most managers we know who fumble MBWA started with good intentions: They wanted to be visible, to demonstrate commitment, to reinforce priorities, to inspect what they expect, and to be helpful. However, their poor execution caused their noble goals to backfire.

1. The "Gotcha" game.

With the wrong tone and an imbalanced lens, all those "helpful pointers" feel more like "Gotcha." It's great to point out what can be done better, along with stories and sharing of best practices, but be sure you're also looking for the good news.

We've seen many managers focus only on all the small stuff that was "wrong" and take for granted what was right. If that's the case, you'll get better long-term results by staying in your office.

2. The drive by.

You come in long enough to make an appearance but don't spend time to make any real connection. These drive bys feel like you're checking off a to-do. Equally destructive is showing up, then heading to a nearby office to close the door and take calls. Wandering around takes time.

3. The high-maintenance prep.

In anticipation of your visit, your employees run around making everything just right. Even if you think you're low maintenance, watch what your employees are doing to prepare.

This is particularly important if your role is in middle or executive management.

It sends a terrible message to the front line when local managers start scurrying to clean up the place or order special food in advance of your visit. A clean work environment is important for the employees every day, not just for your visits.

4. The talking tour.

MBWA is about listening and learning. Sure it's great to reinforce priorities but be certain you're really taking time to listen to ideas and concerns, and to ask what you can do to be most helpful. Listen well, take great notes, and follow up with the people who shared their ideas.

AN MBWA SECRET WEAPON

Which brings us to Monica, a strong, tough, and introverted senior vice president. Wandering around does not come naturally for her, but she's a good leader who deeply understands the value of walking around well.

If her local management team were up for it, she'd ask them to go to the employees' desks to color code their cubes with helium balloons representing something they have accomplished, such as yellow for perfect attendance, red for attaining a degree or certification that year, and white if they were exceeding goals. She also asked her team to be creative and throw in a few meaningful and personal ones, like having a baby.

Now when she wandered around, she had instant conversation starters. Her congratulatory remarks flowed easily into how employees are accomplishing their work and where they need the most help. Plus, the visits felt like an uplifting celebration of the team, not merely making things right just for her.

Your goal is culture, not cat carriers. OCHTC will help you win temporarily, no doubt. But if you want to win well, build an atmosphere of trust and legitimate care for your people. MBWA is a powerful and important way to build confidence and get your team to trust you. Done well, it makes all the difference in the world. Take the time to do it well.

HAVING THE TRUST CONVERSATION

Do you have any trust issues on your team? How do you know? It's not easy to talk about trust. When you want to win well and are ready to hold a deeper trust conversation with your team, here's an easy way to do it.

1. Schedule an hour or so with your team, buy a stack of sticky notes, and grab an easel and some markers.

2. Ask each team member to write down what he considers his most trustworthy characteristics, one per sticky note (e.g., set clear expectations, tell the truth, follow-through). They can come up with as many examples as they like. Don't skip this step; introspection is an important part of the process.

3. Ask each person to share three of her trustworthy characteristics with the group. Some discussion may occur naturally here. Allow that to happen.

4. Have each team member place his sticky notes on the wall or white board, and begin to group them into similar clusters.

5. Identify the themes and write them on the easel paper.

6. Now the fun part: Have the team design the ideal trusted team member. For now this can be just a stick figure with labels, but encourage the team to get creative (e.g., sincere eyes, strong arms for heavy lifting, transparent heart). Name this little guy or gal (e.g., Trusted Tracy).

7. To keep the conversation going, have an artistic team member (or rent some help online) draw up the caricature of your ideal trusted team member (with labels highlighting the characteristics). Laminate the caricature and make copies for your employees to keep.

8. When your team comes together for team meetings or other events, find time to ask who wins the Trusted Tracy award and why. This is a great way for people to nominate and highlight the trusted behaviors that are happening on the team. Team members can do a casual vote to select a winner, and that person gets to hold on to Tracy in his or her cube or office until the next time. This works for virtual teams as well; just take a picture and turn it into an emailable image.

YOUR WINNING WELL ACTION PLAN

1. How, specifically, do you show your team that you trust them?

2. Think of a time when you felt your manager really trusted you. How did you know? How did it make you feel? Who on your team is a candidate for that level of trust?

3. Identify a specific management challenge you face. How can you phrase the issue and share it with your team to get their input and solve it together?

CHAPTER 14

Build a Loyal Team of Problem Solvers

---

*"No problem can withstand the assault
of sustained thinking."*

—VOLTAIRE

When something goes wrong, it's often not the problem itself that's so devastating, it's what happens to an employee's confidence. One of the best ways to support your employees is to help them recover from a bad "last time."

- "The last time I gave someone feedback, he cried."

- "The last time I was honest with my boss, I got a negative review."

- "The last time I presented to senior management, I got so nervous I forgot what I was going to say."

- "The last time I stayed up late working on a report, they didn't even look at it."

- "The last time I interviewed, it turned out the job had already been promised to someone else."

The memory of last time can destroy this time before you even start. In this chapter, we offer specific ways to build, and rebuild, employees' confidence so they get back to performing at their best.

• • •

Even folks who are normally confident sometimes need some extra support.

During the last day of scuba certification, 60 feet below the surface of the crystal blue waters of the Caribbean island of Bonaire, Karin stopped breathing. Oh, air was flowing. But the pristine water suddenly turned dark and crushed her lungs.

Panicked, she signaled to Sven, her scuba instructor, "Up!" He looked confused. Then she signaled more aggressively, "I need to go up now!"

He checked her equipment, looked at her curiously, and gently signed, "No."

Now more frantic, she kicked powerfully to swim up. He deflated her flotation equipment and held her down. Surfacing too soon would create medical problems. He calmly signaled that they would go up together, slowly.

Karin's husband and son watched with amazement. Why was Mom, a former lifeguard, competitive swimmer, and triathlete, freaking out?

Sven knew that how he reacted to Karin's panic mattered. He also knew that he couldn't certify someone who might lose it diving in a remote area of the island. How he responded below and above the surface made all the difference.

Every now and then, the most important thing to do is jump in and take control. Even if that's necessary, it's never sufficient. Sven stayed calm and reassured Karin he was there for her and wasn't going to let her drown. Many managers would have stopped there, or taken over, following up with a conversation about "job fit" once the emergency was over.

It's what Sven did once they got back to the shore that showed his deeper understanding of leadership. After giving Karin the silence of the boat ride back to reflect, Sven gently asked lots of questions to understand the situation. Where had she started feeling uncomfortable? What did it feel like? Were there signs of nitrogen narcosis, an infrequent side effect that makes scuba divers act drunk? Surely such a reaction had an explanation. Before he could support her, he needed to know more.

Then he reassured her that she was still competent. "Karin, you've mastered all the skills and demonstrated them well. You know all the standby emergency procedures. You know what to do."

Next he redefined the problem. "The biggest risk now is that you will be afraid of becoming afraid. You weren't afraid to go deep before, so there's no reason you should now, unless you tell yourself you're going to be afraid."

Sven continued where many managers stop short, with straight talk. "I know you can do this and want to certify you. If you panic again, I can't." There are consequences to low self-confidence. Sven understood that he couldn't risk putting her in a situation where she could harm herself or others, but he didn't just think it, he said it. Only after all of this straight talk did he end on a note of encouragement. "You've got this. Let's go try it again."

They did. The next dive led to certification. Certification led to a wonderful week of diving all over the island, including in remote areas. No fear, just fun.

HELP AN EMPLOYEE REBUILD CONFIDENCE

The difference between energized, productive employees who stay with the team and people who become listless and leave often comes down to confidence. Use the following techniques to help your people rebuild their confidence.

1. Acknowledge what's real.

If last time really was a complete disaster, acknowledge the issue. When you say something "wasn't that bad" but it was, you lose credibility. If they're blowing it out of proportion, offer evidence to help them see the past from a different perspective. Remember, Winning Well managers speak the truth.

2. Break it down.

Ask questions to help them understand the root cause of what went wrong the last time. Chances are, not everything went wrong. It's much easier to improve when you know what to fix.

3. Outline what's different about the scene.

They may think they've seen this movie before, but the truth is, last time was different in many ways. Take the time to explore how today is different from yesterday, or this one's different from that one.

4. Celebrate the learning.

Help them consider all they've learned from the last time. Ask, "What will you do differently this time?" (The wording of the questions presumes that they will try again and helps them realize they have learned something to do differently.)

5. Help them prepare an approach.

The best way to create a win this time is to help them fully prepare. Assist them with questions to nurture their ideas and to help create a strong strategy. To win well, you need your employees to remain confident in their abilities to succeed. Look around. Is there someone on your team who's too panicked to breathe? What can you do to inspire their confidence?

BUILD A CULTURE THAT NURTURES PROBLEM SOLVING

Do you ever wish your people took more responsibility for problems, came up with ideas on their own, and solved problems without always involving you?

When people don't solve problems, there's a good chance the management culture is part of the problem. Some Pleaser and Gamer cultures punish innovation: New ideas have to fight through stifling layers of bureaucracy to be given a chance, or else the slightest "failures" are met with Users' withering derision and criticism. In either case, you won't see much innovation or creativity. It's just not worth it for employees to try.

Even if your company is risk averse, you can create a Winning Well culture that breeds innovation and problem solving with just a few easy steps.

When the World Wide Web was just starting to be used at schools and libraries, David worked for an educational nonprofit and thought it would be fun to put together an outside-the-box research project that the teachers could use with their students.

However, the staff was not particularly computer savvy, and David had only been with the organization for a few months—not nearly enough time to build the relational capital to sell the idea within the company. Fortunately, David took the idea to Jim, the executive vice president, who said words every one of your fledgling problem solvers needs to hear: "Let's try it."

Jim guided David to provide a small demonstration and then make the project available for one or two adventurous teachers who were early adopters. From the first trial runs, David learned how to streamline the project and make it more user friendly. Several staff members took advantage of the project, and David had more credibility in the organization.

Many years later, Jim's words came back to serve David and thousands of young people. During the Great Recession of 2008–2011, he led a nonprofit organization that served young people. You would think the recession might have been a difficult time to do nonprofit work—and you would be right. As happened to so many other contribution-dependent organizations, fund-raising revenue for David's nonprofit contracted as the economy went into a tailspin.

However, during that same time, the nonprofit was able to almost double the number of clients it served. How did it manage that?

Well, it wasn't because of some great idea David had.

Two years prior to the recession, one of his team leaders, Manuel, came to his office and said, "David, my team and I have an idea."

He explained the idea to David. As David thought about it, he considered the lack of infrastructure to support the concept. Scaling the idea would require more staff training, investment in personnel, and resources. It was possible that pursuing the idea would be a distraction from core activities. However, it was very much aligned with their nonprofit's mission, and it had the potential to serve many more young people in a way they needed.

What would you do?

It was then that Jim's words came back to David. "Let's try it!" he said. "Start small—just one location. See how it works." Manuel and his team did just that. They learned some lessons from that one location. Then they rolled it out to several sites, where they learned even more about how to improve the program. Then, just as the recession began, they rolled it out across the organization.

Manuel and his team ended up expanding their ability to reach clients during one of the toughest economies in our lifetime.

To build a culture that nurtures innovation and problem solving, practice these steps:

1. Make it safe to try.

When someone brings you an idea that you've tried before, don't send him away with a terse, "We tried that. It didn't work."

Try this invitation instead: "Thanks for thinking about this with us. We tried a similar idea last year and we found an issue with.... Would you be willing to think about that issue and see if you come up with any ways to make this idea work? I'd love to hear them."

2. Start small.

The technology sector is well known for its minimum viable product practice. What is the smallest way you can test an idea and learn how to improve it? Get moving, get feedback, and get better.

3. Reward behavior, not just success.

This is important. When you ask people to solve problems, you are actually asking them to take a risk. Their solution might not work. How do you respond? Are you grateful they tried, or do you get upset at the failed effort?

To build a culture that nurtures innovation and problem solving, reward effort. Say thank you. Have a prize for good ideas that don't work.

One of the most powerful questions you can ask a direct report is: "How can I help?" The first step is to ask the question. The next is to respond in a way that helps you not only win, but win well.

As a manager, you're in a unique position to help your team in specific ways that no one else can. If you don't ask how you can help, they may not tell you. This doesn't mean you jump in and do their work for them, which might help you win today but wouldn't build long-term competency and sustain results over time. What it does mean is that you:

1. Ensure that your employees have skills and equipment they need to be effective

2. Remove obstacles to success

3. Develop their abilities to take responsibility and problem solve

In our experience, managers struggle with the third one the most: developing their team's ability to take responsibility and solve problems. When an employee struggles to find her own solutions, most managers respond in one of two ways: Users get upset while Pleasers dive in to "help" by offering solutions. Unfortunately, neither response gets you what you want: more time for your work and more responsibility from your team.

If you get upset, they will stop bothering you. They'll also resent you and begin dragging their feet rather than solving problems that need attention. If you play the hero and jump in with answers, the immediate problem gets solved and work continues. But next time an issue comes up, your team still can't figure it out for themselves, and, worse, you've now taught them that if things get difficult, you'll just figure it out for them. They may like you and thank you, but they didn't learn how to do it.

The help your team really needs is not for you to chastise them or solve problems for them. What they really need from you in these moments are your questions.

THE POWER OF HEALTHY QUESTIONS

Managers who win well ask good questions that free up their time by increasing their team's ability to think and problem solve on their own. A good question or two can quickly move the conversation back to the employee owning the problem and analyzing potential solutions. But not all questions are good questions; some can make matters worse.

Poor questions look to place blame and dwell on failure, and they are followed by an implied, "You idiot!" Examples of poor questions are:

- Who screwed up?
- Why did you do that?
- What were you thinking?

In contrast, Winning Well questions focus on learning and on the future to generate ideas and solutions. For example:

- What is your goal?
- What did you try?
- What happened?
- What did you learn from what happened?
- What would you do next time?

Assuming that your staff members have the basic skills, training, and materials they need to do their jobs, this conversation doesn't have to take more than a few minutes.

But what if someone replies to one of your questions with, "I don't know"?

"I don't know" can mean many things. Rarely does it mean the person has zero thoughts about the issue. More often, "I don't know" translates to:

- "I'm uncertain."
- "I don't want to commit before I know where you stand."

- "I haven't thought about it yet."

- "I don't want to think about it."

- "Will you please just tell me what to do?"

- "I'm scared about getting it wrong."

When confronted with "I don't know," Winning Well managers continue the dialogue, easing the person through his anxiety and training his brain to engage. This is where the bonus question comes in. With one question you can reengage the person in the conversation and move through "I don't know" to productivity.

When someone says, "I don't know," ask:
"What might you do if you did know?"

When someone says, "I don't know," your bonus question is: "What might you do if you did know?"

It's like magic.

In our experience, the person who was stymied two seconds earlier will start to share ideas, brainstorm solutions, and move on as if never stuck. It's amazing and hard to believe until you try it.

The bonus question works because it addresses the source of the person's "I don't know." If she was anxious or fearful, it takes the pressure off by creating a hypothetical situation: "If you did know, . . ." Now she doesn't have to be certain or look for your approval, and she becomes free to share whatever she might have been thinking.

If she hadn't thought about the issue or didn't want to think about it, you've lowered the perceived amount of thought energy she must expend. You're not asking for a thesis on the subject, just a conversational reply to, "What might you do . . . ?"

Our brains can do amazing work when we remove the emotional blocks. When you do this for your team, you train their brains to engage, to push through their ordinary blocks, and to increase their performance.

Ultimately, they will be able to have these conversations with themselves and will need to bring only the very serious issues to you.

You'll know you've succeeded in asking healthy questions when a team member tells you, "I had a problem. I was going to come and talk it over with you, but then I thought, you're just going to ask me all these questions. So I asked myself all the questions instead, and I figured it out."

Those are foundational business coaching questions that can work in almost any situation. Of course, there are many other magical Winning Well questions. Here are a few to get you started:

Questions to Address Disengagement

- What is the one thing we could do to make it easier for you to do your job effectively?

- What can I do to help you be more effective in your job?

- What makes you proud—or not proud—to work here?

- What are the most and least engaging parts of your work?

Questions to Build Confidence in Solving a Problem

- What options are you considering right now?

- What do you think are the pros and cons?

- What do you think you should do?

- What is most puzzling or difficult about this?

- What have you done in the past in similar or analogous situations?

- What's your biggest unanswered question about this situation?

- Who do you think has the right experience to help you with this?

Questions to Help the Overwhelmed

- What's something that's very hard for you to do but would really help you be more effective?

- How can I help you right now?

- What people or resources would be helpful to you right now?

Questions to Ask Before Launching a New Project

- Why is this project vital?

- Why are we doing this? Why now? Who will benefit, and what do they most need? How much will it cost, and why is it worth the investment?

- What does success look like? How will we measure our success? What are the process measures that will let us know we are on track?

- Who else must we include? Who do we need to be successful? Who are key stakeholders who should be brought in early?

- How will we communicate? Will we use any online collaboration tools? How frequently will we meet? Will we meet face to face, by telephone, or by video?

- How does this project integrate with other work under way? (In this phase, it's worth going slow to go fast to ensure that there's no redundancy or, worse, competing efforts.) What can we learn from others who've done similar work? (Again, it's worth taking the time to benefit from other people's learning. Breakthroughs are almost always improvements of work that has come before. Be sure you know what that is. Slowing down sets the stage for rapid acceleration down the line, once it's clear who's going to do what and how it fits into the bigger picture.)

- Who will do what, by when, and how will you know? (Too many project teams jump right into the action planning.

Asking the previous questions first will help ensure that your plan is effective.)

Ask these questions and help your team ask them as well. You'll soon find you've increased your team's capacity for problem solving, freed up time to focus on your work, and unlocked leadership potential when you encourage employees who master critical thinking to help guide others through these questions. You're not only winning, but Winning Well.

YOUR WINNING WELL ACTION PLAN

1. Do you have employees who let fear get in the way? How can you best help them develop more courage?

2. Meet with each employee and ask "How can I help?" Visit www.WinningWellBook.com to download a handout you can use to guide you through these coaching conversations.

3. Ask a few of the confidence-building and project prelaunch questions we discussed in this chapter.

CHAPTER 15

Inspire Your Team to Double Productivity

"You've got to think about big things while you're doing small things, so that all the small things go in the right direction."

—ALVIN TOFFLER

---

ommunicating the big picture is a skill that's often lost in management-development programs. After all, big-picture thinking is for execs, right?

No. Everyone needs to know how the pieces fit together, where they fit in, and why their work makes a difference. In this chapter, we'll share some secrets to getting your team connected to the bigger mission.

• • •

When David was 16, he told his father he wanted to be a vegetarian.

"That's great!" his father replied. He jumped up from the couch, went to his file cabinet, and pulled out old magazine articles and copies of nutrition guidelines.

His father was a vegetarian. The articles he gave David discussed how to balance amino acids and other nutrients. David studied those articles and got started. He was a strict practicing vegetarian.

For three days.

So, you can imagine David's reaction when his 16-year-old daughter told him, "I want to be a vegetarian!"

She followed through on her desire, and for several years now, she has not eaten any meat.

What do you suppose was the difference between David's short-lived experiment and his daughter's lasting lifestyle change?

Let's start with David. Why do you think he wanted to be a vegetarian?

You might think it was because he wanted to be like his father.

Nope.

The simple truth is that in his warped adolescent brain, he figured that being a vegetarian would somehow help him get a date.

Now contrast his shallow motivations with his daughter's reasons. She wanted to live a more sustainable, less impactful lifestyle; didn't want to inflict harm on other sentient creatures; and wanted a healthier diet.

The difference in their behavior came down to one thing: their reasons why.

Her "whys" were deep, compelling, and lasting. David's were shallow, short-lived, and easily accomplished in other ways.

Now think about the work you ask of your people.

The activities you just thought about, that's their "what"—the reports, the phone calls, the meetings, the manufacturing, the customer service, the planning, the calculations—all the stuff we do.

The "what" is certainly important, but the issue starts with a deeper question: "Why?"

In fact, this question is so vital, so full of life, energy, and potential that we can confidently say it is the most important question you can ever answer for your team.

This isn't a question about great metaphysical or philosophical dilemmas. It's about the most practical question every team member needs to be able to answer.

Simply put: Why are they doing what they're doing? Managers who win well connect the "what" to the "why."

If you've ever seen the classic 1967 movie *Cool Hand Luke*, in which Paul Newman's character serves time in a prison chain gang, you'll remember the ditch scene.

The jailers force Luke to repeatedly dig and refill the same ditch.

The meaningless labor is designed to break his spirit. When you don't connect the "what" to the "why," you condemn your team to soulless drudgery.

Is your staff doing work disconnected from real meaning or purpose?

If so, there are two possible reasons: (1) they don't understand the "why" behind the work, or (2) there is no legitimate "why."

"Whats" without "whys" are a waste. They waste time. They waste energy. They waste your people.

Every task performed by every person should serve the mission of your team, work group, and organization. If it does not, it needs to be challenged, reexamined, and a better way found, or the task should simply be eliminated.

When you say, "I believe this matters and here's why . . . ," you provide clarity, hope, and purpose, but you also create an opportunity for your belief to be challenged, which could be just what is needed to open meaningful dialogue.

Every single task performed by every person should serve the mission of your team, work group, and organization. If it does not, it needs to be challenged, reexamined, and a better way found, or the task should simply be eliminated.

Otherwise, you've sentenced your team to do work meant to break their spirit.

DOUBLE THEIR PRODUCTIVITY

Winning Well does not require you to be a cheerleader in business clothes, full of rah-rah with a fake smile. That's not what inspiration looks like for anyone paying attention. Inspiration comes from connecting people to meaning, purpose, and their own ability to succeed.

In fact, in just five minutes per month, you can inspire your people and increase their productivity by simply asking them to think about various "whats" and asking, "Why do we do these things?"

Don't treat this activity as a quiz. Treat it as a mutual exploration, a chance for all of you to discover together why something matters.

In just five minutes, you will discover a renewed sense of purpose; people will sit up taller, smile, and have pride in what they're doing. Sometimes participants in this activity even get choked up as they rediscover the meaning in their work.

If you don't like the answers you discover, that's okay. If your "why" is all about you (e.g., "I'm doing this for more money, power, or prestige"), you are right to be concerned.

People aren't stupid.

When it's all about you, they'll suspect you're a User, and you can expect them to do only what they have to do. People work best when their work has meaning. Despite the selfish behavior that perpetuates in organizations, few human beings are truly motivated by making their boss a hero.

If you examine your big "why" and the answers are shallow, vapid, and uninspiring, take the next step. Where can you find meaning? Why is the work important? How does it contribute to a bigger picture? If it does not, can you take steps to eliminate those tasks?

Start with "why" and then be sure to see how your team's work fits into the bigger picture.

DID YOU GET THE GUITAR?

Karin had promised to take pictures of her son's last marching band performance during his senior year of high school. She raced into the parking lot, grabbed the camera, threw her high heels in the back seat, and raced down the grassy hill.

To her relief, the band was just lining up on the far side of the track surrounding the football field. The sun was beginning to set, which she knew would make for perfect lighting.

She set up the tripod, adjusted the telephoto lens, and got some great shots: the mellophones doing their sideways stunt, some up-close head shots, she even made sure she got some great ones of his friends.

She immediately went home to upload them to Photoshop for fine-tuning before he got home. As soon as he walked in the door, she proudly played him the slide show.

"Mom, did you get the guitar?"

"Huh? Ben, you play mellophone."

"Mom, the band moves into a fantastic formation. It looks like a guitar right in time with the music. Did you get a picture of that?"

"Oh boy, no, I didn't." Without thinking about how it would make a great management story later, she had completely missed the big picture.

It happens on teams too.

Lisa was the project manager for a large-scale six sigma project. The phone rang; it was one of her managers, Tim. "Lisa, you know that project you asked me to look into? Well, all the milestones are on track. IT, HR, Operations, everyone has met their deliverables, but the results are still in the toilet."

The project looked good on paper, but results weren't moving.

The big picture was messy.

He finished with, "We have to stop thinking about this as a project. We need to step back and figure out what needs to be done."

Tim was right.

WHY WE MISS THE BIG PICTURE

Sometimes we get too close and put our heads down doing tasks. There is danger in looking at a project in isolation. We miss the big picture because we:

- Follow a template

- Focus on tasks over root cause

- Don't ask the obvious questions
- Followed directions blindly
- Are afraid to say it's not working
- Don't talk to one another
- Don't have the right plan
- Don't have the right metrics built into the plan
- Are overly focused on doing
- Are working too fast

WHY MANAGERS FORGET
TO CONNECT THE DOTS

If you undercommunicate the big picture, it could be for one of the following reasons:

You Don't Fully Understand It

❏ Let's face it: Sometimes the big picture is murky. It could be that change is happening so fast it's hard to keep up. Or there's a lot of secret activity behind closed doors, and what's hitting the front line really doesn't make sense.

❏ If what you've been asked to have your people do feels stupid, it's important to ask the right questions to ensure that it makes sense to you. If you're frustrated and confused, your team will see it. Get the clarity you need first. When that is politically difficult or your boss interprets clarifying questions as resistance or becomes defensive, try putting your question in terms that help him or her. For example:

❏ "I understand you need us to do 'x' and we'll get that done. I also want to make sure my people and I fully comprehend the reason 'x' is important. Can you help me understand how this plays into the big picture so we're able to do everything you need?"

❏ If it still doesn't make sense, respectfully articulate your concerns. You may have a perspective that has yet to be considered. For more on working with difficult bosses, see Chapter 22.

You Rely on Someone Else to Do It

❏ You know your team has heard the message at least four times. Go for six. Even if they've heard the webcast, participated in the town hall, read the company newsletter, and had a visit from the senior team, they need to hear it from you.

❏ People often need someone they trust to translate the big picture. They need time to ask questions and to voice their concerns. Just because they smiled happily when your boss's boss shared the news does not mean they understand and are ready to go.

You're Too Busy

❏ When you're drowning, it hardly seems like a good time to step back and contemplate the big picture. But you may be surprised how much time you can save by making such a little investment.

THREE WAYS TO COMMUNICATE THE BIG PICTURE WITH EASE

Try these three steps to improve your ability to connect people to the bigger picture:

    1. Magnify the Meaning—Talk to your team about the impact their work has on the greater good: the customer, the world, and others they serve. Engage in dialogue and ask them to identify what makes them most proud about the work they do.

    2. Clarify Priorities—It's vital that the work you ask people to perform doesn't feel like a random list of unrelated tasks. Bundle the work into meaningful chunks that link back to the bigger picture. If you can't combine the tasks into meaningful clusters, you may have too many priorities. Figure out what matters most and nail those. Know what you will drop if you run out of time; if you have to fail at something, be sure you're the one who chooses what that will be.

3. Simplify the Message—If you can't explain your team's mission in one sentence, you don't fully understand it. If you're really struggling, ask a few strong team members to give it a shot. Everyone on your team should be able to describe your team's mission in a similar way.

All the other work you do as a manager is undermined if your team doesn't have a strong unifying sense of where they're headed. Ask your team today: Can they articulate their mission in one sentence?

YOUR WINNING WELL ACTION PLAN

1. Articulate your work group's mission in one sentence.

2. Ask each employee to articulate why he has been asked to do the work a certain way. If he struggles, use that as a window to open the "why" conversation.

3. In a team meeting, ask your team to identify any tasks they are performing that they feel don't add value or aren't aligned with the mission. Then take time to discuss the alignment or eliminate the tasks.

CHAPTER 16

Get the Feedback You Need and the Influence You Crave

"I remind myself every morning: Nothing I say this day will teach me anything. So if I'm going to learn, I must do it by listening."

—LARRY KING

---

ometimes your employees will make it difficult for them to be heard. Ironically, when they most need to talk, they'll push you away with behaviors that will make your hair curl. If you can take the high road, meet them where they are, and run along beside them, you may be surprised how much you can hear. You'll gain a reputation for Winning Well, versus that of a soulless User, Gamer, or Pleaser.

• • • •

Karin was arguably the most disengaged and lazy sorority pledge at Wake Forest University. She had rushed because she was warned that nearly all of the social life on campus centered on the Greek system.

The difficulty was that she had trouble viewing herself as a "sorority girl." She was more of the studious, madrigal-singing type.

She started skipping mandatory events because they felt like a colossal waste of time and blowing off requirements to interview every sister about her favorite foods and secret fantasies. When her advanced biology class started to crush her brain, she began work on her exit strategy.

When Brig, the president, pulled her aside, she felt instant relief. She wasn't going to have to quit. She was going to get kicked out—even better.

"Karin, you seem athletic. Do you know how to roller skate?"

Taken off guard by the seemingly random question, Karin remembered childhood summers when her friend Sabine visited from Germany and they would lace up their roller skates to race, swirl, and make up shows every day until dusk.

"Actually, I do," she confessed.

"Great, we need someone to do the roller skate leg of the relay around the quad for the Greek games." (Think high-energy, silly, yet serious Olympics.)

"Oh, I'd love to, but I didn't bring my skates to school." Off the hook again.

"Oh, I'll find you some skates."

"Well, I'd have to try them out, and I'm so busy studying for this biology exam." Even she knew how ridiculous that sounded as the words spewed out. Clearly she was still trying to get tossed out.

Brig persisted. "What time are you done studying tonight?"

"Midnight."

"Great, meet me on the quad at midnight. I'll bring the skates. The race is at 3:00 p.m. tomorrow."

As Karin laced up the skates, Brig asked her she if she liked the sorority. At last, a window to confess. She skated, and Brig ran beside her on the moonlit quad. Karin poured out her fears of losing the academic scholarship she needed to remain at the school if she didn't pass biology. She explained her resistance to the interviews and her feelings that this just wasn't for her.

Brig listened intently and asked questions. "Why did you join the sorority? What requirements make this seem impossible? Do you know why we require you to talk to each sister?"

She explained the "why" behind every ritual. And then worked to co-create a reduced schedule of obligations that Karin could commit to and keep her academic standing.

When Karin returned for homecoming a few years later, she asked Brig if she remembered that midnight meeting. "Of course I do," she said, smiling. "Good leadership is never accidental."

"How crazy is it that I ended up being president?" Karin asked.

Brig looked at her full of confidence and pride. "Karin, I knew one of two things was going to happen with you. You were going to quit, or you were going to be president someday. My vote was for president."

INVITE FEEDBACK

People in positions of power often sabotage themselves and create environments where no one will tell them the truth—often difficult truths about themselves.

Mark's Story

Mark was a leader who had just crashed and burned. He was the president and CEO of a midsize hospital and called us after he had made a decision that could cost him his reputation and maybe his job. He had promoted a woman who subsequently embezzled and then tried to sue when the hospital finally terminated her employment. After her termination, it was clear that many people in the organization had known she had problems for a long time.

Mark stared at the floor, his jaw clenched in frustration. He looked up, and with a quiet whisper asked, "Why didn't anyone tell me?"

The sad part was that it didn't have to happen this way. His people knew it wasn't a good call, but he never heard their feedback.

Watching Mark's behavior in meetings was painful. He would ask for input on a question, and if it didn't match what he hoped to hear, he would cut off his employees, telling them they didn't understand, or that the rationale behind their suggestion wasn't important to him. In meetings he was firmly caught in User behaviors, valuing his own confidence above humility and myopically focused on results to the exclusion of the relationships that could have kept him out of trouble.

However, he also had a Gamer tendency to anoint certain employees as "golden children" who could do no wrong. Mark was charismatic, and people would work hard to gain his favor, often by criticizing people they knew he didn't like. Two of his direct reports, including the woman who would embezzle, had learned how to tell him what he wanted to hear, and he lavished praise and promotions on them. Frankly, it was surprising anyone shared any feedback at all. As we worked with the staff, we repeatedly heard the refrain, "Why bother? Mark doesn't want to hear it, and he's just going to do what he wants to do anyway."

Mark was caught in the quicksand of User and Gamer behaviors. Driven for results without regard for all the people he needed to achieve them, he fostered division and backstabbing competition between his employees rather than productive collaboration. Throughout the organization people worked not to improve patient outcomes or financial health but to get his approval. Over time, Mark had isolated himself from hearing the truth he desperately needed, and people justifiably gave up trying.

Every manager can fall prey to Mark's tendencies. Here are six ways to ensure you have the truth you need and to keep your reputation for Winning Well:

1. Ask for the truth.

Regularly encourage dialogue in your team. Ask people to teach you one thing you don't know. Become a person known for caring what's really going on.

2. Say thank you.

When someone shares a hard truth, especially about you, thank him or her for having the courage, taking the time, and caring enough to share it with you.

3. Respond.

If you ask for input, take time to respond. Even if not every idea is actionable, acknowledging that the ideas were heard and considered increases the likelihood that you will hear more in the future.

4. Never ever shoot the messenger.

If someone has the heart and courage to bring you a difficult truth, even if you vehemently disagree, bite your lip. If you attack her, she will probably never bring you another concern.

5. Find your truth tellers.

There are people who understand their team, environment, or processes and are willing to voice their observations. Find these people, keep in regular communication, and let them know you value their observations.

6. Look in the mirror.

If you suspect you are not hearing the truth from those around you, it is time to look in the mirror and examine how you are interacting with others. We would bet you're having difficulty with one or more of the first four items on this list. If you struggle to see it, ask others for input, find a mentor, or consider a coach.

HELP THEM DEVELOP THEIR VOICES

Have you ever been in a meeting where two people said exactly the same thing, but one person was heard and the other was not? Have you ever been on a conference call and felt like you were speaking to the mute button?

This happens to your employees as well. It could be with one another, or in other meetings they attend. Help them develop their skills so their voices can be heard.

Lisa was fortunate early in her career to have a great mentor on being heard. Her company had hired a consultant to do some important process work. Lisa was still in her 20s, the youngest person in the room by over a decade, and also the token HR person on the project—not the best combination to be heard. But she was fired up and passionate about treating employees with respect, transparency, and engagement.

The first few times Lisa shared her opinion, she was ignored.

The consultant pulled her aside on a break and said, "Everything you say is right on, but they can't hear you, your timing is off. Here's the deal: When I give you the look, you start talking employee engagement. I will back you up and ask provocative questions for them to consider."

It worked masterfully. They heard her, and the project members started to care for the people side of the project. She paid close attention to the timing of the consultant's nods and learned the patterns so she wouldn't require the prompts.

THE VOICE APPROACH

If your employees have trouble being heard, work with them to organize and articulate their thoughts using the VOICE approach.

V—Visualize

Visualize what you are going to say and how you are going to say it. Include it all: the eye contact, sitting up tall with an open stance, strong projection, and confident tone. Visualize the listeners' receptive response. It's much easier to feel confident when you've practiced.

O—Organize

Organize your thoughts in advance. Make an outline if needed. Consider the key points that will support your point of view. Know your opening sentence so you won't be tempted to start with an apology ("This may be a bad idea, but ... ").

I—Inquire

If possible, do your homework in advance and find out other people's opinions on the topic. If you're responding spontaneously, ask for feedback (e.g., "How do you think this idea could impact our project?").

C—Consider

Listen carefully to other peoples' opinions and ideas. Thank them and respond appropriately. Build on and integrate their ideas if possible.

E—Energize

Breathe out from deep in your body. Your body will naturally draw in breath and release tension. Speak with full breath—avoid the 'too cool for school' gravely vocalization. Stay energetic in your delivery. It's hard to ignore someone who is genuinely passionate about his point of view.

Most important, be sure you believe what you have to say. If you're unsure, your audience will be equally skeptical.

BUT WHAT IF THEY DON'T LISTEN TO ME?

"But I've told them!"

Lenny was a passionate but frustrated manager in a human services company. His people weren't implementing new procedures that would improve client service and reduce costs. When we interviewed Lenny's team, it was painfully obvious that they did not understand the new procedures and were not clear about how they would help the people they served.

When we shared the results of these interviews, Lenny's frustration was obvious. He echoed the cry of managers the world over: "But I've told them! I swear I have. I can even show you the meeting agenda where everything was spelled out."

Have you ever felt like Lenny? One of the most frustrating aspects of being a manager is when your employees won't listen to you.

- You passionately share a vision of the future, and are met with chirping crickets.

- You share new procedures to help improve results, and everyone continues doing what they've always done.

- You make recommendations grounded in clear facts, and they are ignored.

How you handle these moments matters. Learn from them and your effectiveness will skyrocket, but if you become so frustrated that you rely on fear or power, your credibility (and soul) will vanish. User managers often go on rants and throw in a few threats about what will happen if their people continue to ignore them. Pleasers may beg, cajole, and then move to attack with, "What's wrong with you guys?" Either way, you may get compliance for a little while—a short-term win. However, the score is now: you 1, your team 0. They feel diminished and stupid. They lose confidence in you and won't tell you when they're confused or something is unclear. They may even look around for another job with a manager who knows how to communicate.

Here are ten questions to ask when you feel like your team won't listen:

1. What do you really want?

Whenever you have management challenges, the first thing to examine is your own motivation. Are you truly focused on results and relationships, or are User or Pleaser motivations creeping in?

There's a big difference between wanting what's best for the team and wanting what's best for you. So what is it you really want?

If the answer is submission—"I know what's best, and they'd better listen to me"—then you won't ever have a team that wins well. They will act out of fear when they have to and ignore you when they feel it's safe.

When you want more—for the group to succeed together, to make an impact—you're on your way to Winning Well.

2. Do you speak their language?

Do the words and concepts you use mean the same thing to your team that they mean to you? Do you share numbers and facts when stories and demonstrations are needed—or vice versa?

3. Do you listen?

If you don't hear what people tell you, they'll naturally think you don't care, they'll lose heart, and they will stop caring. To learn whether or not you're hearing people, ask a few team members to share with you: "Is there anything you've been trying to tell me that I'm just not hearing?" Be quiet and listen. Thank them for sharing, and respond in time. You don't have to agree, but you do need to hear. It takes both internal values of confidence and humility to truly listen without defending yourself. When you listen, you strengthen the connection with your people and learn what areas of training, execution, and accountability need attention.

4. Do you have credibility?

If your team can say, "You don't know what you're talking about," and they have evidence to back up their conclusion, expect to be ignored. Credibility is built, not demanded. If you don't know what you're doing in a certain arena, admit it and seek out others with the expertise to supplement what you do know. When your people can't trust you or rely on you, but you insist on compliance, you fight an uphill battle you cannot win in the long run.

5. Do you know what matters to them?

Everyone values something. If the values you promote conflict with your people's values, you'll have trouble being heard.

6. Are you ordering or inviting?

Invitation is the language of collaboration. We don't mean the literal phrasing of the words (although that can make a difference too), so much as the attitude behind them. People know when you focus on relationships along with results. Do you communicate that you're better than everyone else and they should serve you? Or do you invite people with mutual dignity to participate with you?

7. Have you explained the "whys"?

Even military briefings include the reasons and objectives behind the orders. Sometimes people's lack of response results from not understanding the consequences of their action or inaction. This is one area where Lenny was able to improve. He had shared the new procedures, but without connecting the "what" to the "why."

8. Do you check for understanding?

An idea is rarely as clear to the listener as it is to the speaker. Use the check for understanding tools from Chapter 4. Ask your listeners what they heard, what they understood you to be asking, and what they understand the consequences to be.

9. Do you say it often enough?

This was the core of Lenny's problem. He had shared the new procedures and he had the meeting agenda to prove it, but when it comes to communicating change, once is never enough.

We have worked with so many frustrated leaders who complain that their team is insubordinate or unresponsive. When asked if they communicated the issue to their team, they say yes. Here are a few of the answers we got when we asked, "When was the last time you communicated the issue?":

- "Last year."

- "At that off-site the year before last."

- "We were in the hallway six months ago."

- "At the staff meeting last month."

- "In an email."

If you've communicated something once, you haven't communicated. Your people have lives beyond you (we know—the truth hurts) and may have bigger fish to fry than your company's vision. Users and Pleasers often think that something they said two years ago, or even two months ago, is on everyone's mind when they wake up every morning, but that's foolish and only leads to frustration. Managers who win well communicate frequently.

10. Do you say it in different ways?

People learn differently—some by seeing things, some by hearing, some through practice, and so on. As you practice communicating frequently, use different techniques. Try our Winning Well 6x3 communication strategy: repeat critical information at least six times through three or more channels. For example, to communicate a new procedure, you might use email, a staff meeting, and one-on-one meetings for your three channels.

David once visited the company headquarters of an international medical technology firm. In a single gathering of staff, the leaders of the organization used heartfelt letters, humorous skits, a spoken address from the president, call and response, and audio-visual production, and they fielded unscripted questions from attendees. In that one meeting they used every item on this list, and theirs is frequently cited on lists of best places to work.

If you feel as if no one's listening, ask yourself these ten questions, be honest with yourself, and take action in response to your answers. Winning Well managers master these challenging communication moments.

If you've communicated something once,
you haven't communicated.

YOUR WINNING WELL ACTION PLAN

1. What are three ways you could make it easier for your employees to tell you the truth?

2. Which employees could benefit from the VOICE method? Schedule some time to share and discuss the model with them.

3. Brainstorm the tough questions that might be on your

employees' minds and proactively answer them, questions such as:

- Why do we do it this way?

- How's our company really doing?

- Why didn't you ask us?

- Why is _____ not dealt with?

- If I speak up, will it hurt my brand?

- Do you think I'm ready for a promotion?

- Why is there so much turnover ?

- How can we get past this feeling of constant crises?

CHAPTER 17

Energize Your Team and Ensure That They Own the Results

"When he took the time to help the man scale the mountain, lo, he scaled it himself."

—TIBETAN PROVERB

When your team comes to you and asks, "What should we do?" they're often asking something much deeper. Answer that deeper question and you will build confidence in your people, grow their skills, and free up more of your time.

• • •

The wind shifted, the mainsail swung over the boat, and the deck leaned until David found himself staring at water where the horizon used to be.

The skipper called out instructions: "David, trim the jib...more tension!"

He grabbed the winch handle and began to crank clockwise, hoping to feel tension.

Nothing.

The line moved, but he wasn't sure if it was enough.

He cranked it in the other direction, looked back at Patrick, the skipper, and asked, "Which way should I turn it?"

Patrick's next words were a powerful leadership moment, but they didn't answer David's question.

At least, not the one he had put into words.

What's the real question?

You might wonder what David was doing controlling tension on a sail when he wasn't sure how to do it. Hadn't he been trained?

The answer is yes, but ....

He had gone sailing in the San Diego Harbor with several of his colleagues, including their skipper, Patrick Maurer.

Before they left shore, Patrick oriented them to the sailboat, explained the vocabulary, gave them instructions, and ran them through the roles they could play. David sat next to the winch that managed tension on the front sail (the jib).

Before they left the dock, Patrick was very clear about how everything operated, especially the winch. He had even spelled out the answer to the question David would ask later as the boat leaned precariously: The winch could be turned in either direction.

So David knew he could turn it either way; what was it he really wanted to know?

With the boat leaning and seven other passengers counting on him to tighten that line, what he really wanted to know is the same thing employees often want to know when they come to you for answers:

- "Am I doing this right?"

- "Am I going to be okay?"

- "What do you really want?"

If you're like many managers, when an employee asks a question for which you're confident she's received training, it can be frustrating.

You might think, "She knows this! Why is she wasting my time?"

We invite you to look a little deeper. In a very short time, you can give employees what they need and grow stronger, more productive team members.

HOW TO ANSWER THE RIGHT QUESTION

When David looked back over his shoulder and asked, "Which way should I turn it?" Patrick calmly, but firmly, replied, "You can turn it in either direction. One way is easier; one way is faster."

Did you notice what Patrick didn't say?

He didn't answer the question David asked. David wanted something straightforward—right or left—but Patrick didn't just tell him. Instead, he used a coaching technique called reduce ambiguity. He gave David information that he could use to make his own decision. (Given that they were tipping and David was looking down at the water, he chose the faster but harder option.)

Patrick's words answered David's underlying question: "What do you want me to do?" while also giving him the ability to make that decision for himself next time. From now on, Patrick would be able to spend his time on other aspects of running the sailboat.

And there was something else.

In addition to the words he spoke, there was the way he spoke them. Calmly. Firmly. His tone answered David's other underlying questions: "Am I going to be okay? Am I doing this right?"

Patrick's tone said, "Yes."

Don't give them the answer they want and neglect the answer they need. Empower your people to achieve by answering their bigger question.

Don't give them the answer they want and neglect the answer they need.

INCLUDE THEM IN
THE JOURNEY

Meet Simon, a call-center director supporting the business customers of a global telecom company. Quality was what mattered most for these valuable customers. So from Simon's perspective, the new system the company had designed was genius. Instead of customers typing their service orders in an email for employees to retype into the systems (which almost always contained errors), the customers now had an easy systems interface that would flow through to the backend systems.

The new approach was faster and provided higher quality and an added bonus: It worked on weekends. There was only one problem: The employees (and their union) hated it. And they had a point.

"What about white glove treatment for high-end customers?"

"What about relationships?"

The union steward, Kenetra, was adamant that the change was "just proof" that management cared about the bottom line more than the customer experience.

In truth, both Simon's and Kenetra's points were valid. Customers wanted efficiency *and* differentiated service from well-trained employees like Kenetra.

It wasn't either/or. It wasn't management or the union. They needed to work together to build a customer-focused adoption strategy that the reps could believe in.

In Chapter 14 we talked about the powerful question, "What might you do if you did know?"

There's a related question that works well in times like this:

"What would it look like if this system was great for customers *and* employees?" Follow that question up with one more: "How can we do it?"

These questions get everyone working together toward a positive vision and looking for solutions. In this case, both the union and management had a common goal: to improve the customer experience. Kenetra was honest about the union's fear of lost jobs. Simon was honest about his concern over wasted time and productivity.

They outlined the benefits of the new system that they could all agree to and brainstormed the best use for the freed-up time.

They finally agreed that they would use the system to reduce the retyping work and instead train the service reps on more value-added tasks to create deeper connection with the customers. These behaviors would make customer relationships last longer and lead to future sales and the additional union work that would come with it.

Breakthrough results require every heart and brain working together to achieve results. Change requires confidence and inclusion, not selling. When you can take your audacious vision and make it feel real, practical, and achievable, your team will sail along with you.

1. Establish a clear vision.

Be crystal clear about what you want to accomplish. Communicate and reinforce your vision through every medium possible. When you're sure everyone's got it, communicate even more. It's important to explain the reasons behind a change as well as to identify the specific behaviors you need from employees in each role.

2. Be honest about the benefits.

The notion that all that employees care about is WIIFM—what's in it for me?—is BS. Sure, employees want to know what's in it for them. They equally want to know what's in it for you and for their customers.

In the absence of information, people often jump to the most pathological conclusion. Leave out key information and they fill in the blanks with assumptions (e.g., the next thing you'll do is downsize). They want to know that you've thought this through with your brain and not just your pocketbook.

3. Start small.

Don't advocate for an idea or change that's half-baked or full of flaws. Test it first with a small group, take their feedback seriously, and get it right. It's tough to regain credibility. "Oh yeah, I admit it stank before, but now it's better," only leaves people wondering why some bozo made a choice to sing praises for an idea, system, or process that was full of problems in the real world.

Even if it looks great on paper, your boss is sold, and it worked well in the IT war room, field test the change first.

Yes, this takes time. Go slow to go fast.

In the previous example, Simon and Kenetra worked out the kinks with one team and gave headquarters feedback until they were sick of hearing it. Take the risk of making some waves to make it easy for your team. This office was slower out of the gate than most regions, but no one remembers that part of the story because they got it right in the end.

4. Establish easy-to-access listening posts.

This is perhaps the most important part. Really listen to what your people tell you. Most important, respond to feedback with solutions, not selling. When you fix something, communicate it back using the 6x3 methodology.

5. Leverage reluctant testimony.

Share as many testimonials as you can, especially from people who were doubtful at first. Get your most excited employees showing how your new idea, system, or process changed their world. Your most influential stories will come from the least likely suspects: the sales guy who never bothered with this stuff before, the new rep who's now running circles around the old-timers because she uses the new system, the supervisor who got his entire team (including the union steward) performing acrobatics with the system.

6. Involve the team in key decisions.

No one wants stuff done *to* them, or even *for* them. *With* them goes a lot further. Ask employees, "What's working well and how do we leverage it? What enhancements do we need? Where should we head next?" All these questions go a long way. Include employees by involving them in your change efforts.

INCLUDE EMPLOYEES WHEN THE GOING GETS TOUGH

We've talked about how to include employees in a change effort, but what about when the going gets tough? Is it appropriate to include them in your angst?

It depends. Even when you think you're buffering them, you may be transmitting more stress than you think. Unexplained angst in the eyes of your leader can be more stressful than knowing what's up. When the issues aren't confidential, managers who win well use the problem-solving tools from Chapter 8, define the challenge at hand, and ask their people, "How can we solve this?"

WHAT ABOUT THE "TROUBLEMAKERS"?

Jane knew she needed to include her employees in more decisions, but every time she brought up an idea up for discussion, Sam shot it down. He had lots of opinions and no filter. Meetings always lasted longer than needed, and the minute he opened his mouth, the eyes started to roll.

Jane got to the point that when she saw him coming her way, she did everything she could to look busy and avoid conversation.

Perhaps you've got your own Sam. Most teams experience a "troublemaker" from time to time. We've found three troubles that arise in these situations with troublemakers:

Trouble Number 1: They Create Negative Energy

Unchecked troublemakers may create a negative drain on a positive team. They can dominate meetings. Others may try to stand up to them for a while but give up when it just eggs them on.

Trouble Number 2:
They Bring Out the Worst in Your Leadership

After a while, these troublemakers may wear on you too. When you are under pressure, you may lose patience. You may stop listening. You may react in a negative way.

Trouble Number 3:
They May Be Right

These "troublemakers" may be loud and frustrating, but they are often right. The real trouble is they are often worth listening to. Beneath all that noise and confusion are often salient concerns worth checking out with the rest of the team.

Tips for Taming the Trouble

Here are some techniques we recommend to tame the "trouble-makers":

- Validate their feelings—ensure that they feel heard.

- Take it out of the meeting—don't engage in debate in front of the team.

- Schedule private time to hear their ideas.

- Give them a specific, productive role on the team.

- Keep them challenged—ask them for solutions.

- Recognize their successes.

- Provide space to talk about other issues they may be experiencing.

A FUNCTIONAL CONVERSATION
ON DYSFUNCTION

We like to use this exercise during a group's formation to get folks talking about common experiences and appropriate remedies as early as possible. This conversation also provides a safer environment to surface important dynamics a mature team needs to share without direct confrontation. It also works well to surface and discuss concerns in a group that's experiencing conflict.

Step 1

Give every team member sticky notes. Ask them to identify the behaviors that (in their experience) most get in the way of results or team progress. It's important to explain that this is based on a lifetime of experience, not just this team. Then ask them to write one behavior on each note.

Step 2

As team members are ready, have them bring their sticky notes to a wall or whiteboard and begin to organize them into clusters. Enjoy the banter as the clusters form.

Step 3

Circle the most frequently listed dysfunctions.

Step 4

Take the top few categories and invite the team to say what they would do when faced with such scenarios. Encourage them to share stories of best practices they've used in the past.

Step 5

Develop a set of standards or team norms for how such issues would be addressed if they were to occur on this team. It's very important for teams to talk about their own dysfunction. But early in the process, it may be easier to talk about standards and stories to establish a framework of desired behaviors.

The discussion alone will often help employees self-correct. At a minimum, the inclusive standards make it easier for you to hold future individual or team discussions if the behavior continues.

YOUR WINNING WELL ACTION PLAN

1. Ask your team to write down or print out a few questions they have that they're afraid to ask. Collect them in a way that protects privacy and answer them in a team meeting.

2. Identify three steps you could take to better include your team in accomplishing your most important goal.

3. Try the sticky-note exercise we just described to get your team talking and establishing standards of behavior.

CHAPTER 18

A Powerful Prescription for Energy- and Soul-Loss Prevention

"Life is too important to be taken seriously."
—OSCAR WILDE

Work can be fun, but should it be playful? You might be thinking:

- Work is not fun; that's why they call it work.

- Play is not good for my leadership image.

- Sometimes, in the right context.

We invite you to consider an alternative. Laughter is a signal of organizational health. It doesn't mean your company becomes a circus; it's an indicator that people are healthy, enjoy their work, and can be their most productive. This is one of those key places to focus on the "and" above the "or." Winning Well managers get results *and* relationships; they have fun *and* get the job done.

• • •

Karin had just been promoted to manager and head swim team coach of her neighborhood pool. She and her staff had spent the week brushing algae off tiles, making bulletin boards, and organizing schedules. They were ready for the launch of an amazing season.

She locked up her bike and unlocked the gate, a bit nervous; she was excited to lead the first practice of the season. The kids arrived, and after a few complaints about the extra cold water, jumped in to begin their warm-up.

Suddenly, sweet "6-and-under" Ned splashed and screamed like he'd seen a shark. "Miss Karin, Miss Karin, Come quick! I saw a fish!"

"Ned, calm down, you didn't see a fish. Put your head in the water and keep swimming," Karin replied, knowing that she needed to stand firm to keep her credibility as a new coach who was not much older than most of the swimmers.

Just then, her assistant coach, John, who had gotten in the water with the kids to show them it couldn't be *that* cold, pulled himself out the pool and came running over. As he dripped on her sweatshirt, he whispered, "Uhhhh, Karin. There really is a fish."

She quickly got everyone out of the pool and discovered that there was not just one fish, but three. The kids all jumped back in and tried to chase them with their bare hands. Ned ran home to get his fishing rod.

The phone rang.

It was Peter, the head coach of the rival swim team. "Just calling to congratulate you on your first day as head coach and pool manager. How's it going?

"OMG, there are fish in my pool!" As soon as she said the words, Karin realized who had put the fish there.

Well played.

A great start to a great season. Their rivalry turned from competitive angst to collaboration and real friendship. Now, you may be thinking, sure that stuff works for lifeguards but not in the corporate world. Or, you know, he was probably flirting with her, right?

Well, actually it can work in the corporate world. We both have seen humor and fun work as a powerful prescription for soul-loss prevention. And, yeah, in hindsight he probably was.

PLAY FOR RESULTS

We both get to work with very different companies with unique cultures. One company Karin worked with developed a Jimmy-Fallon-meets-training-videos way to keep their reps up to speed on breaking news and key initiatives. It's funny, upbeat, engaging, and, most important, sends a clear message about key priorities.

The videos stream live to employees' computers every few days, and people look forward to the next edition. After watching a short segment, reps know what's important and what to do next.

Their chief operating officer said that one of the managers who plays the "anchor" is normally very serious and results driven. She's glad to see him leveraging the lighter side of his personality to engage these young reps. He's a well-rounded manager using all his strengths. Results are on an amazing upward trajectory.

When employees have fun, they are more creative, more connected, and less stressed.

One telecom sales team launching the Droid phone rented professional *Star Wars* costumes for the management team, which drove hundreds of miles visiting their retail locations to fire up the local sales reps and create intrigue for customers. It inspired the team and the customers loved it.

We've both worked with clients who organized citywide scavenger hunts to reinforce organizational purpose while giving everyone a chance to have fun, work with different people, and problem solve together.

And we've both known executives willing to dress in costumes, change the words to a song, grab a microphone, or do a rap. Of course, this is not every day, but a sprinkling of play can go a long way. It's refreshing to see managers have fun with their teams.

One client was told that having such fun could damage her "authority" with her team, that she should laugh with them less and keep a professional distance. She thanked the feedback giver (remember to respond to feedback with a "Thank you") and kept on playing, but with a more careful view of who was watching.

You see, their results were skyrocketing in the middle of what appeared to be an impossible challenge. Their laughter had a powerful uniting quality. Her ability to play while focused on results caused her team to respect her more, not less.

She learned to take on a more serious stance when visiting headquarters, but when they were in the field where the real work gets done, she kept up the ruckus.

SILLY SELLS

Perhaps the riskiest use of strategic silliness we've seen was by Robert, the chairman of an international company. Robert's company was pitching a new client on a highly strategic project. Robert's team had all traveled quite a distance to discuss this important deal that would lead to solid revenue and potentially open the doors for significant work in the future—nothing to play around with.

The potential client, Lynn, was impressed with the company but had some valid concerns. Robert began with a serious expression commensurate with the importance of the meeting.

He began, "I know you'll be very impressed with what you see here today. We've got a great track record of results, and numbers to back it up. I can't wait for the team to share more about our programs. But before that, I've written you a little song."

He pulled out a piece of notebook paper with the song he penned, and began to sing. His a cappella serenade included why Lynn should give them a shot. The mood was instantly lightened by his silliness. Her guard dropped a bit.

He sang.

She listened more deeply.

After applause and laughter, Robert's team launched into a highly professional presentation with data, video, tours, and sitting side by side listening in on calls. They proved they were the best. Lynn hired them. Not because of the song, but not in spite of it either. Silliness has serious benefits. Robert had done his homework: He knew Lynn appreciated fun songs and so came prepared to have productive fun. Well-timed silliness can:

- Break the ice

- Show you're real

- Show you're bold

- Energize the meeting

- Showcase creativity

- Build relationships

- Create memories

STRATEGIC SILLINESS PRECAUTIONS

After her standing ovation to Robert's song, Lynn responded: "Great stuff. *Never* do that at our corporate headquarters." They both grinned knowingly. To be effective, these types of silly and fun activities:

- Must be timed well, with a receptive audience

- Work best with kindred spirits

- Can't stand alone (surround them with great results and execution)

- Work because they're unusual and infrequent

- Are tasteful

Humor and silliness are powerful energizers when done well. However, approached the wrong way, they can suck the life force out of an employee so fast that it's difficult to recover the relationship.

When Play Goes Too Far

Gary, the president of a Fortune 50 company, had been talked into doing a karaoke night as part of an off-site management meeting. Gary is about as straitlaced as you can get. We can't imagine he has ever sung karaoke in his life. In fact, we're pretty sure that his vision of hell includes being asked to sing at work. The only explanation for this choice of team builder could be that some executive coach convinced him that this would show his lighter side and help him connect with his team.

Gary stood with his back pressed against the farthest wall from the microphone, sipping a diet soda. Everyone could see his discomfort, which of course was contagious.

In an effort to ease the situation, several of Gary's vice presidents started coaxing their teams to sing. Renee, one of the more outgoing managers, was approached by her boss. "I know you can sing; go help Lisa," who was one of Renee's peers.

Now, Renee knew that Lisa had already had one too many chardonnays.

"What's she going to sing?" Renee asked.

"'You Gotta Fight for Your Right to Party!' You, know, the Beastie Boys."

Renee stopped her and didn't give it a second thought. About a year later, Renee's boss brought up the incident as evidence that she needed to be a better team player.

Don't Play to Patch Problems

You can't play or team build your way out of fundamental problems. We hope you don't ever say, "People are upset; we need to do something fun."

No, you don't. You need to solve your communication problems. Or fix the process issue that's preventing people from doing their jobs.

Play is like the icing on a good cake. It makes good things sweeter, but it's no substitute for the cake itself. Imagine trying to spread frosting over a mushy, half-baked cake. It's impossible, and you'd end up with a sticky mess.

When there's a problem, fix the problem. Then have fun together.

When there's a problem, fix the problem.
Then have fun together.

When the Powerful Prescription Turns into a Dangerous Drug

Recently, David was at a family party, a baby shower, and broke one of his own rules.

When someone said something poking mild humor at herself, he piled on with a comeback at her expense. Everyone laughed or took mock offense, as he had hoped, but afterward he wished he hadn't said it.

In this case, he'd tried to be funny at the expense of his own mother.

At some point, most of us use irony, sarcasm, or jokes at others' expense. For many, it's a part of their family or organizational culture. We rely on this type of humor for several reasons:

- We want to feel better about ourselves, either by making ourselves look clever or diminishing the other person.

- We want to cover insecurity, another form of trying to feel better about ourselves.

- We indirectly try to address a real issue. Rather than speak directly about a difficult subject, we use sarcasm or negative "jokes." Chaucer and Shakespeare both point out the use of jesting to speak truth.

- We protect ourselves. Some people use sarcasm to push others away or avoid their own fear or pain.

- We don't know how to do anything else. We lack the skills to address issues effectively.

If you want to influence other people, using sarcasm and humor at others' expense is full of problems. Bottom line: As a manager, this type of humor will undermine your mission to win well. Here are just a few of the problems with using sarcasm and jokes at others' expense:

1. It creates shame in the target.

2. If you shame a person when you have positional power, you have put that person in a difficult fight-or-flight position.

3. You get the opposite of what you want. A very skilled, self-aware person might come and talk to you about it, but another person might find a way to "get even"—perhaps resorting to similar "humor," undermining you, reducing the amount of work he does, or stealing.

4. You give permission for everyone to do it. Before long, your clever comeback has turned into a caustic workplace where negativity reigns. (At the extreme, this can even cause human resource problems with hostile work environments.)

5. It doesn't build anything. You might make someone stop doing something by being sarcastic and shaming her, but you'll never create a new positive behavior this way.

6. You limit creativity. Consistent sarcasm creates an atmosphere where no one will try a new idea. The risk of failure and incurring shame is too great.

7. It drains energy. We do our best work when we're in the zone—feeling competent, challenged, and ready to do our best. Sarcasm and humor at another's expense create doubt and negative energy.

8. It destroys trust.

HOW TO AVOID HUMOR PITFALLS

When you want to use humor, ensure that it will resonate and not make the situation worse with these five strategies.

1. Start with results.

When you're tempted to use sarcasm, stop and ask yourself what you really want. What results are you looking for? Encourage, inspire, teach, coach, demonstrate—these are always more effective than using sarcasm.

2. Address issues directly.

Never use humor to deal with behavior or performance problems. As we've seen, it creates more problems and does nothing to help the situation. Address these issues directly and professionally.

3. Use humor effectively.

Any comedian can tell you there is always one safe target to make fun of: you. Self-effacing humor displays humility and tells your people that you don't feel like you're better than they are and that you don't take yourself too seriously. It builds trust because people know you own your problems and understand your shortcomings.

4. Deal with your own junk.

If you're carrying around hurt or insecurity and regularly mask it with sarcasm or making fun of others, take some time to reflect on what's going on there—maybe work with a coach. If it's deep, talk with a counselor.

5. Clean up.

If you have potentially hurt others in the past, apologize and make it right.

When teams come together and have a strong sense of identity, they can often start to pick on others who are outside their team. Maybe it's the competition or a team in a different department. As a group, poke fun at yourselves but resist the urge to joke at others' expense.

We love to laugh, and we need far more of it, but if you're a manager or seeking to influence others, avoid sarcasm or making fun of anyone (except yourself) and watch your credibility grow.

YOUR WINNING WELL ACTION PLAN

1. Do you believe in play at work? Why or why not?

2. Think back to times in your work life when you've had a good

laugh. What happened? Was the experience planned or sponta-neous? How can you create similar opportunities for your people?

3. How do you maintain humor in your team without it turning negative?

4. Plan a time for you and your employees to go have fun together. Pack a picnic lunch and go bird watching (yes, we actually know a sales director who did this with much success). Have your team write leadership spine poems, which involves building a short poem using only the words written on spines of books and placing them in a stack. Even better, ask your team for suggestions about what would be most fun.

5. Take one of your key initiatives and find a fun way to talk about it at your next staff meeting. Write a limerick, dress in a costume (Karin's father dressed as his key initiatives at work every Halloween for several decades), or sing a song (just no Beastie Boys, please!).

CHAPTER 19

Great Relationships Require Great Results

It's easy to make excuses, particularly when others are skeptical. We've both experienced times when naysayers told us to lower our expectations. One or the other of us had been told not to expect:

- People to embrace a new process

- "Those" people to be able to perform at that level

- To sell that product in that rural market

- To get that job without direct experience

- To make an impact too quickly

- That kind of motivation to work in a union environment

- The vice president to wear that costume

- Those famous writers to respond to my email

And the people who told us these things were wrong. Professional relationships thrive in an environment of high expectations and excellent results. In this chapter you'll receive a variety of tools to ensure that your expectations are sufficiently challenging and to provide your people the confidence to reach them.

• • •

It was one year since Christine had been handed the challenge of managing an inmate-run clothing factory at a state men's prison. This wasn't a scene from *Orange Is the New Black*. As one of only a few female staff members and lacking any supervisory experience, Christine was in a tough place and skeptical about the assignment.

However, Christine's factory ultimately outproduced the prototype operation, had an impeccable safety record, and could run itself without supervision. David interviewed Christine to find out what made such a rapid transition possible.

"It began with my belief in the people. When they came to me, they wanted to tell me about what they had done on the outside—why they were in prison. I cut them off, told them I didn't really care about who they were last year.

"I told them, 'This is who we are going to be in this factory, and this is what we're going to do.' Most of them didn't believe it at first, but pretty quickly they responded to someone believing in them."

She went on to describe how the inmates would initially object to sewing because they thought it wasn't something men did. Christine would walk over to one of the industrial sewing machines, quietly operate it, produce a garment, return to the men, and say, "You're telling me women can run this industrial machine better than you men? I don't believe that."

Christine met them where they were, even though she might not have agreed with their chauvinism. She challenged the men to be more than inmates, to become better men and achieve more than they thought was possible, and they did.

Christine's magic worked because she truly believed in their potential for contribution. She refused to see them as their past and truly believed in the possibility of a bright future. If she had not believed it, neither would they.

Before you can challenge your employees, you must be sure you're up to the challenge.

Great results start with thinking bigger. Great results require audacious goals. Great results can't happen if you doubt they are possible.

Your employees need you to be the visionary, to think bigger than they can imagine. Otherwise you're just a group of people muddling through. Our FAST model can help you organize and move to greater results in less time.

THE FAST MODEL
FOR BIG RESULTS

To get results fast, use the Winning Well FAST model to focus your efforts.

F—Focus

To move results quickly, focus is key. Resist the urge to fix everything. Identify and communicate the biggest priorities and break the work into manageable tasks. Focus on what each team member needs for success.

Align on two to three key leadership messages to share in every context. Communicate them to the point where it feels obnoxious, then communicate more. Check for understanding. Communicate again. Test it by asking, "What do you think I most want to talk about today?" If they don't shout out the priorities, you're not clear.

Make big work small. It's tempting to build action plans with lots of activity to show you are trying. Less is more. Too much action overwhelms and confuses. Identify two to three actions that will make the biggest impact and hit them hard. Reinforce with focused and consistent leadership messaging.

Use data to get surgical in your approach. Know the outliers and give them focused recognition and support. Avoid broad-brush interventions. Focus just-in-time actions on those who need them.

A—Acknowledge

Slow down early and listen to concerns. Stop to acknowledge progress.

New initiatives are almost always piled onto an existing workload. Acknowledge conflicting goals and competing priorities. Listen carefully to concerns. Prioritize. Give permission to stop. Some balls must drop. Decide which ones.

When you're moving fast, don't forget to pause at progress. Acknowledge small wins. Celebrate new behaviors. Recognize breakthrough thinking.

S—Stretch

Fast-paced change provides great growth opportunities. Stretch yourself and others. Provide special projects and stretch assignments. Turn strong players into teachers. Ask everyone what they must do next to achieve.

Stretch people to try new behaviors. Stretch boundaries, assumptions, and rules. Spend time asking, "What have we never tried before?" Engage people who bring different backgrounds and perspectives from outside the team.

T—Think

Go slow enough to think about what you're doing and who you're involving.

Every fast-moving project contains elements of stupid (e.g., time-wasting tasks, old processes, and reports that no longer align with a new vision). Empower everyone to say "Stop" as needed.

Carefully measure progress and fine-tune as needed. Watch for unintended consequences. Be ready to change course as needed.

When moving fast, it's easy to exclude. Think about peripheral players who must understand your plan. Slowing down to include the right players early leads to smoother acceleration.

THE POWER OF EXPECTATIONS

When David was an elected city councilman, he watched the amazing power of expectations instantly transform the conversation.

When city government faced a contentious decision, there were often three or four groups involved. The professional city staff with their interests, the elected officials (who rarely agreed), contractors, and the public would frequently reach logjams—even when everyone generally agreed that change was needed.

These groups would get stuck. "What are we going to do?" they would ask each other. Somebody would propose a solution, and it would get shot down: "Oh, we can't do that."

After a few minutes of this, the mayor would say, "We can find a thousand reasons why this won't work. That's not the question. For the next ten minutes, let's just answer this question: How can we get it done?"

That question presupposed that a solution was possible and that they could accomplish their goals. Not surprisingly, they did. In the time it takes to snap your fingers, that one question and the belief it communicated were all they needed to break the impasse.

That's the power of a positive expectation and belief in what the future can be.

Expect more and watch your people's energy lift as they rise to the challenge.

HOW TO SET CLEAR EXPECTATIONS

Setting clear expectations requires deliberate effort. Here's a process to ensure that you're communicating exactly what you expect.

1. Get clear on your own expectations.

If you're not clear on what you want, we guarantee you won't be able to communicate it. We've both worked for the person (perhaps you have too) who could never articulate just what he wanted. He just knew it when he saw it—and he rarely ever seemed to see it.

The lack of clear expectations always resulted in rounds and rounds of frustrating iterations wasting everyone's time and weakening respect along the way. Don't be that guy, or you'll drive your folks crazy.

2. Engage in conversation.

Be clear about what you want, but also listen carefully to concerns. Better to identify expectation disconnects as early in the game as possible.

3. Write them down.

In most circumstances it's useful to write down agreed-to expectations. This works one-on-one and with teams. The process of writing down expectations often leads to further clarity and serves as an objective reminder as expectation violations arise.

4. Check in.

From time to time it's useful to check in. You can easily draw a box with four quadrants to guide the conversation (you can download the worksheet from our website, www.WinningWellBook.com). Just above the box, write "What I expect," and just below it write, "What I don't expect." Outside the left side write, "What I get," and outside the right side write, "What I don't get."

First, each person, including you, completes the matrix, jotting down areas where expectations are being met and where they are not. For example, in the top left quadrant, each person writes down what she expects and gets from the other person. In the top right, each person writes down what she expects that she doesn't get, and so on.

Next, discuss areas of agreement and areas of concern. What does each person completing the matrix expect that he does receive, or doesn't expect and doesn't receive? Take time to discuss each quadrant of the matrix. Start with appreciation for what people expect and do receive. Recognize the good and then identify the gaps or the disconnects and discuss.

Finally, identify specific actions that would enable you to work more effectively together.

HELP THEM TASTE THE WIN

What if you believe your audacious goal is achievable, and you've set your clear expectations, but your team is skeptical? The next step is to help them taste the win. One of the best ways we've found to do this is to isolate one or two needed behaviors and then spend a day making it really fun to try them out. We call this powerful technique confidence bursts.

The idea is to create a full-court press of the given behavior to prove what is possible at individual and organizational levels.

Build a temporary scaffold of support around employees with lots of extra attention, skill-building, fun, recognition, and celebration. The risk is low—it's just one day and it doesn't feel like a big commitment to change. Once people experience success with the behavior, their confidence improves and the ceiling of what they perceive as possible moves a little higher.

Every time we've have done this, the results have been head turning and remarkable. The best part comes in the afterglow discussion: If you (and we) can make this much magic on this day, why not every day?

We find that a few sets of these intervals spaced one month apart can lead to remarkable and lasting results.

You'll know the behavior has sunk in when the impact of these "burst days" begins to dwindle but the overall results stay high. The behaviors have become so frequent that the extrinsic motivation is no longer necessary. The value in the behaviors has become an intrinsic choice.

HOW TO HOLD A CONFIDENCE BURST DAY

Here's a step-by-step process for creating a confidence burst day.

1. Pick one or two tangible skills to work on.

2. Schedule the special day and create anticipation.

3. Begin the day with energy and fun; make it feel like a holiday.

4. Set specific, measurable goals that can be achieved that day.

5. Hold training and focused skill building throughout the day.

6. Have your team members with the most expertise in the skill you're working to build work side by side with those still learning.

7. Celebrate every little success in a big, public way.

8. Communicate specific success stories, including the "how" behind them.

9. Celebrate and debrief at the end of the day on what worked differently this day and what was learned.

10. Begin the next day with a reminder of key learning.

ARTICULATE RESULTS

Of course, once you get the results, it's important to have the confidence and ability to explain them.

Pete was a retail store district manager. His district was performing well, but his store managers would inevitably fall apart every time a senior executive visited a store unannounced. Although nothing was wrong with the stores, the managers would get so nervous they'd clam up, misspeak, or babble on about inconsequential minutiae. Pete's credibility was taking a hit.

Many people in Pete's position would have gone into self-preservation mode, invested longer hours to show up more and more in the stores, thrown in a few ultimatums, and given any manager with a bad visit a documented warning. But Pete knew that although that might get their attention, what these managers needed most was confidence. He didn't just want to win, he wanted to win well. Reacting with longer hours and ultimatums would have had the opposite impact in this case.

So Pete came up with the Green Jacket Effect. He began practicing with the team. He'd have all the store managers take turns visiting one another's stores wearing a really ugly green jacket. The jacket triggered a simulation of an executive visit.

Whoever was wearing the green jacket was to be treated like an executive visitor. Which of course had the side benefit of that person thinking like an executive: interpreting trends, asking great questions, knowing what BS answers sound like.

The store managers practiced telling their store's story. The more they practiced, the less nervous they became. Soon they could explain their results and articulate their action plans, and give shout-outs to recognize high performers.

Of course every business is different, but being able to explain your results and talk about your business is an important skill for any manager to master. Here are some tips for when you need to share your results. Use these ideas during executive visits, for presentations to boards, and when delivering presentations to other managers.

- Greet the executive or other visitor proactively with a firm handshake (demonstrate that you're glad she came).

- Proactively explain your numbers and the reasons behind them.

- Start with your opportunities and articulate key actions.

- Share your creative approaches to implementing key initiatives.

- Introduce the visitor to other employees, and share something unique that each person does.

- Recognize a few people for their outstanding contributions—things that make people say, "Wow!"

- Talk about your challenges and how the visitor can help.

- Share ideas for improved processes and say how you are pursuing them.

- Take active notes on all suggestions.

- Send a thank-you email summarizing all follow-up items.

THE BIGGEST CHALLENGE OF ALL

Sometimes the best way to challenge your people is to get out of the way.

Meet Chang, a millennial high-school orchestra director. It was the last concert of the season. The seniors wore roses and beamed with the energy of folks getting ready to start on a new adventure.

Chang held up his baton, and the music began. Powerful. Brilliant. Exciting—an energetic send-off to the next phase of their lives.

Then he looked at the orchestra and grinned.

He stepped off the podium stage right, folded his arms, and watched from the sidelines. Five measures later, he looked at the audience, smiled with confidence, and walked off the stage. He never came back.

The orchestra continued. Powerful. Brilliant. More exciting. The audience sat mesmerized by the leadership moment. The students didn't miss a beat. They were performing—without their leader. Or were they?

Chang had left the stage confident that:

- The vision was understood

- They had a game plan

- They were accomplished players

- They had practiced

- They would listen to one another

Chang's confidence said:

- I believe in you.

- You're ready for the next phase.

- It was never about me.

- Go be brilliant.

No conductor—just audacious confidence, high expectations, and a willingness to get out of the way.

YOUR WINNING WELL ACTION PLAN

1. Test your goals and expectations for the team. Are you doing everything you can to challenge the team to achieve more? Are your expectations clear? Use the expectations exercise described in this chapter with your team to discuss how expectations are, and are not, being met.

2. Which of your employees could benefit from a deeper one-on-one conversation on expectations?

3. What are three ways you can get your employees to help one another improve like Pete did with his green jacket?

CHAPTER 20

Sustain Your Team's Energy and Momentum

"Instruction does much,
but encouragement everything."

—JOHANN WOLFGANG VON GOETHE

Have you ever witnessed the exuberant celebration during an employee-recognition event when a name is called and the whole audience seems to scream, "Yes!" People rise to their feet. It's high fives the whole way back from the stage. The congratulations go on all night. When the recognition is on target, everyone feels fantastic.

We've both been involved in lots of recognition situations over the years. We've been recognized. We've engaged in hundreds of conversations about who should be recognized. And we're confident that you already know you should encourage your team and show them your gratitude and appreciation.

We're confident because you've almost certainly been taught by parents, teachers, or other leaders to say thank you. You learn these lessons early in life, and yet many leaders struggle to do it well.

• • •

Karin and her husband had arrived at a ritzy hotel for a friend's wedding. Parking was tight so they drove around the corner to the back of the building.

Right beside the dumpsters were several tables set up for a hotel staff recognition luncheon. The nicely printed signage thanked them for their commitment to customers, but the thank-you signs were not enough to hide the trash or disguise the smell.

Karin was floored. She thought:

Let me get this right. You're event superstars. You work to make every bride's and corporate meeting planner's dreams come true. Have you ever suggested a bride hold her rehearsal dinner by the dumpster? What in the world possessed you to put white tablecloths on a backdrop of trash? What other options did you explore? Do you seriously expect the folks you're "recognizing" to come back in and create magical, creative moments for your guests?

Someone must have thought this was a great idea, but it's more than the thought that counts. It's the impact.

And then there's Sherika, who can tell you what it feels like to be on the receiving end of dumpster recognition. Sherika's manager rushed into her office, told her how wonderfully she had done, that she should be so proud of what her team had accomplished, and then rushed out just as quickly. Sherika sat there, speechless and upset—because it wasn't her project.

This manager had intended to encourage her but was so clueless about what Sherika had done that his "encouragement" was insulting.

Or maybe you've been there and experienced the eye rolling and slow hand clap when the wrong name is announced at an awards banquet. A quiet murmur comes over the audience and you watch the text message "WTF?" start to flow.

And finally, there is the leader who thinks (or says), "Why should I have to encourage people? This is their job, isn't it?"

We received a strong answer to this question from Jennifer, a former store manager at a national women's clothing chain. Jennifer is outgoing, incredibly gifted at making customers feel comfortable, and was considered to have high potential by her district and regional managers. Within a year of being promoted, however, she had quit. A few months later, she ran into her district manager at a coffee shop. As they talked, the district manager expressed surprise that Jennifer had left. "You were one of the most talented, capable managers we had. You had so much to offer and you left. Do you mind if I ask why?"

Jennifer told us, "It took me a few moments to recover from the shock. The district manager had never shared any of those positives with me. I got a weekly, sometimes daily, breakdown of where I wasn't good enough—and that was it."

Jennifer told her former district manager, "I thought I was failing. I'm shocked to hear that I was doing anything right. I wish you had told me I was talented or capable at the time."

How much lost talent, energy, and productivity will a lack of encouragement cost you?

WINNING WELL FUEL TO SUSTAIN YOUR TEAM'S ENERGY AND MOMENTUM

Human beings need encouragement. It's a fact of life. You get more of what you encourage or celebrate and less of what you criticize or ignore. If you want a team that doesn't need to be encouraged, get a cat. Otherwise, if you're working with people, they need encouragement.

You get more of what you celebrate and encourage;
you get less of what you criticize or ignore.

Remember, Winning Well management is a relationship, and the quality of your relationships depends on what you invest in them. As with most of the Winning Well practices, once is never enough.

If you're married, imagine what would happen if, after your

wedding, you never said "I love you" or never held hands or kissed the other person. You couldn't expect your relationship to last very long.

That's the equivalent of never saying thank you or encouraging your team members. Yes, it's their job insofar as they've made a commitment to your company, just like spouses make a promise to commit to one another. That doesn't mean you should take that commitment or your team's work for granted.

This doesn't have to be difficult. When a team member shares an accomplishment:

- Celebrate with him.

- Ask him what he likes most about his accomplishment, what the most challenging aspect was, what he is most proud of.

- Explore the positive consequences of what he's done.

- Offer to share his accomplishment with others (and respect his wishes with regard to public acknowledgment either way).

- Smile. Clap. Cheer. Ring a bell. Do whatever is sincere for you.

As we mentioned at the beginning of this chapter, encouragement can be challenging for some leaders. Many leaders, especially those who are driven and focused on results, have a hard time encouraging their teams. The good news is that you can follow a few principles to ensure that your people receive the encouragement fuel they need to keep Winning Well. Let's start by looking at why recognition so often backfires.

REASONS RECOGNITION BACKFIRES

Recognition matters, but recognition can also backfire. It's important to understand the impact.

1. Recognizing every little thing.

You might hear someone say, "There's no such thing as too much recognition." We disagree. As parents who praise their kids for every little thing at every turn may create dysfunction, shallow praise over the small stuff can be a real turnoff for your serious performers.

One manager we know instructed team leaders to say, "Thank you for coming to work today," as a way of reducing absenteeism. If showing up is the best behavior you can find to recognize, keep looking. That doesn't mean you never acknowledge people for their consistency, but to do so every day cheapens it.

2. Recognizing with caveats.

Examples of recognition with caveats include:

- "You did an awesome job, but ...."

- "Your performance was amazing, except for that hiccup in the second measure of the song."

- "You were very friendly with that customer, but you gave her the wrong information. Keep up the great work."

Recognition is recognition. Coaching is coaching. Both are necessary, but when you confuse one for the other, it can quickly demotivate your people.

Note: The only time to use the sandwich method of placing criticism between two compliments is when the person has approached you and asked for feedback. Otherwise, your criticisms negate any praise you might have shared, and people see you as disingenuous.

3. Recognizing in a way that creates discomfort.

Some people hate the spotlight. Even the thought of being called onto a stage is enough to make some A-players break out into hives. Others love the attention and are disappointed when the recognition is done privately where there's no one to applaud. Everyone needs recognition that is meaningful to him or her.

4. Recognizing based on numbers, while ignoring the behaviors.

In an effort to remain "objective," many leaders rely heavily on numbers and rankings as they select whom to recognize. Overreliance on the numbers can be a slippery slope. If a backstabbing team member wins an award, your entire recognition program loses credibility, and you send a message that the ends always justify the means. A good way to overcome this is to identify additional behaviors or related metrics to use as gateways.

5. Recognizing the leader without acknowledging the team.

Leaders need recognition too. Sometimes there is huge value in recognizing a leader in front of her team. However, this is risky and must be done with care. Many times it's best to use big recognition forums to recognize team efforts and save the individual leadership kudos for another venue.

6. Recognizing a big deal as if it's a small deal.

Or recognizing a small deal as if it's a big deal. "Thanks for saving us $5 million; here's your certificate," can backfire. Ensure that you calibrate the level of accomplishment with the level of recognition, and ensure that all the leaders delivering recognition at the same event are aligned with one another.

7. Recognizing in a sloppy way.

We've both seen leaders go to the podium and read off a name of someone they've been called in to recognize, only to mispronounce the name. This mistake seems really basic but happens far too often. It doesn't help if you laugh first and apologize. When you get a name wrong, you undermine any value your presence or praise might have had. You've just told the person he's not important enough for you to bother learning his name. If you're the big shot called in to shake hands, be sure you take the time to learn how to pronounce names.

8. **Recognizing by reading from a script.**

In our opinion, the managers who go to the microphone without lengthy notes always win. They speak from the heart. So what if they can't quote every number? Their eyes light up. They tell a story. They mean it. Make sure you understand the recognition enough to mean it.

With those eight mistakes out of the way, let's take a look at three principles you can follow to make sure your encouragement does what you intend.

TRAITS OF EFFECTIVE ENCOURAGEMENT

In order to provide healthy encouragement that fuels performance, focus on three traits. Make sure the encouragement is:

Relevant

Specific

Meaningful

Relevant

Let's start with what you should encourage. Think about the encouragement mistakes we just discussed. Many of these mistakes arise when managers encourage the wrong behaviors.

One of the questions we frequently hear from audience members is, "Why are there so many poor leaders in our organization?" There are several answers to this question, but one of the most common is that leaders at every level can reward behaviors that don't contribute to teams Winning Well. (These leaders often reward behaviors that helped them or their team to win once, but not well, and not over time.)

Have you ever had a supervisor who congratulated you for doing something that you knew really wasn't praiseworthy, or worse, something you knew was actually detrimental to the organization in the long run? We've seen many managers pile praise on an employee while the other team members rolled their eyes and said to themselves, "If you only knew . . . ."

The first key to make encouragement work for you and your team—to be the real fuel of Winning Well—is to ensure that your encouragement is relevant to the work.

Encourage what you want.

What are the specific things people do that contribute to healthy relationships and meaningful results? Encourage those things that are relevant to the relationships and results you want to achieve.

Which brings us to Leslie.

Leslie was performing a newly created organization-effectiveness role. Her team would be called in to assess a situation, make recommendations, stay late, and roll up their sleeves to support implementation.

One day there was a big awards reception where one after the other, managers whom Leslie and her team had supported were called onto the stage and celebrated for their tremendous improvements and accomplishments. No one mentioned her team or the work they had done.

After the ceremony, Leslie pulled her boss, Ray, aside and blew a gasket. "No one knows we were involved in this! How are we going to build a reputation and a brand if no one knows what we do? How am I going to get promoted if I'm always working behind the scenes?"

Leslie was sure this was the wake-up call Ray needed to get working on their brand, but he just looked at her calmly. "Why do you do this work?" he asked.

"Because I believe our employees deserve a better work environment, and that better culture will lead to improved customer service."

"I see. Are you sure?"

Ray had her there.

He continued, "Look, I know how hard you work and the impact that you make. You have to trust that when the time comes, the right people will understand your contribution. If you can't trust me to do the right thing, you might be working for the wrong guy."

Leslie felt awful. She did trust Ray, and she did care about their work. He was right in pointing out that her behavior wasn't aligned with her stated intention. She was winning, but not well. Her confidence was strong and needed some humility for balance.

And then he did something Winning Well managers do so well: He sat in silence for a moment and let her think.

Ray then broke the uncomfortable silence with, "Okay, so from now on you and I are going to be like Will Smith and Tommy Lee Jones from *Men in Black*. We will know our work is done when the situation has improved, the chaos is gone, results are under control, and no one remembers we were ever there."

Now *that's* a brand.

Ray was wise and had encouraged the behaviors he wanted. He kept Leslie focused on what actually mattered (the game) and not on the accolades (the score) that may have felt good but weren't their real work. Leslie eventually did receive the recognition she had hoped for in the form of a big promotion. That felt great to her because it was a testimony to the value her and her team's work had on the organization.

Specific

You've taken the time to identify your team's relevant behaviors. Now, when you acknowledge them, be specific about what you encourage. Describe what actually happened and why it was important.

Ineffective: "Hey, Bob, great work!"

Effective: "Hey, Bob, I really appreciate the extra hours you put in on that project last week. The customer was happy with the results and renewed his account. Thanks again for the extra effort!"

If you can't describe the actual behaviors, you're not ready to offer encouragement because you don't know what people did and they won't know what to do again. When you take the time to get specific, people know you understand their work, and you reinforce positive contributions.

Meaningful

Effective leaders know that people are different. They want encouragement in different areas, and they receive encouragement in different ways. As you saw in the list of mistakes, encouragement can cause discomfort when it's not meaningful to the person being recognized. In contrast, meaningful encouragement is relevant to the work and to the person. Here are six ways to make recognition more meaningful.

1. Customize it.

Find out what is meaningful to each member of your team before the time comes to recognize. The easiest way to do this is to ask. Make it a part of your onboarding checklist. When someone joins your group, simply ask, "How do you like to be recognized for a job well done?

2. Personalize it.

Everyone likes to feel known. Just a little personalization can go a long way. Some people like time off. Some people like a chocolate bar. Some people like public recognition. Some people hate public recognition. Sometimes it's a simple pat on the back. Are your employee-appreciation gestures really just "more work"? Don't do that (unless you know for certain that it's something your people like).

One best practice we've seen is to take your team out to Starbucks (or bring their favorite drinks to them). Be sure to get the itemized receipt and write each person's name next to his or her drink. Put the receipt in your recognition folder and wait a couple of months. Then, when an employee does something worthy of a caffeinated high five, bring him his favorite drink. Simple, cheap, and personal goes a long way.

Another meaningful idea that communicates your commitment to your people is to buy your team copies of a leadership, management, or professional development book to start the year. Personalize each book with an inscription thanking the person for something specific he did the year before along with inspiration for a project ahead. The key here is to make the inscriptions highly personalized and mention something specific he's done that added real value. It's a way to show that you pay attention, appreciate what your people do, and invest in their career. In response to these personalized books, we've consistently received comments like, "I've never had a manager who paid so much attention to who I was, what I was doing, and invested in my own personal success."

3. Make it timely.

When someone does something awesome, she knows it. There's no better time to show that you know it, too, than when the endorphins are still flying high. Slow down enough to say, "Wow, that was amazing—thank you," even if you plan to do something more formal later.

4. Encourage strengths.

Encourage people on the aspects of their work that they find meaningful. Some people pride themselves on making the deadline, others on getting it right, and still others on building a team to achieve results. Acknowledge the work they did in the area that is meaningful to them. People appreciate it when you acknowledge their strengths.

5. Align it.

Meaningful encouragement is also aligned with other organizational behaviors. For instance, it doesn't come across as authentic when you tell an employee, "You're amazing—I don't know what we would do around here without you!" at the same time you give everyone on the team a raise—except for that employee. Make sure words and actions align with organizational behaviors.

6. Make it meaningful for the team.

Finally, be sure to acknowledge the team as a whole. When you acknowledge individuals in front of the team, talk about how their actions contributed to the team and helped everyone to win.

It is easy to get caught up in your day-to-day challenges and neglect your team, but the best managers and leaders know that encouragement fuels their team's performance, energizes team members, and keeps everyone focused on what's most important. Remember: You get more of what you celebrate or encourage; you get less of what you ignore.

YOUR WINNING WELL ACTION PLAN

1. What was the most meaningful recognition you've ever received? What made it special?

2. What do you appreciate most about each member of your team? Write it down. When's the last time you told them?

3. What are the specific behaviors you want to recognize? What do people do to contribute to relationships and results?

4. What story best exemplifies why you want to recognize someone?

5. How does each person on your team like to be recognized for a job well done?

6. What could you do this month to ensure that each member of your team knows how much you appreciate her? How will you make this recognition and encouragement relevant, specific, and meaningful?

CHAPTER 21

Essential Practices That Build Your Credibility and Influence

"There are some things you can't share without ending up liking each other."
—J. K. ROWLING

Your ability to win well and produce lasting results through healthy relationships depends on how much influence you have with your people. Influence is not the power to make people do things. Influence only comes through credibility—the extent to which your people know you, believe you, trust you, and respect you.

• • •

Karin had just been promoted to her first big leadership position in human resources, concurrent with a significant merger at Verizon. All the "important" players were new. Karin had a new boss, a new team, and new senior leaders to impress. Life can be messy: She was also going through a divorce and trying to pick up the pieces in a new life, in a new home, as a single mom. She lived in Baltimore, and the job required substantial travel to Manhattan.

One of the first tasks in her new role was to build a diversity strategy. She gathered a "diversity council" representing each business unit to collaborate on the strategy and plans. The work they were doing was vital. She was convinced she was nailing her new role.

Until . . . .

A woman from her diversity council burst into Karin's office, pointed her finger at her, and yelled, "You're a fraud!" Karin couldn't imagine what she was talking about. She was deeply hurt by the remark from this trusted teammate.

The woman continued, "I came by your office yesterday to drop something off when you weren't here and saw the pictures on your desk. They're all of you and your son—no dad. You lead all these meetings where we work on programs to make it easier for single moms and *not one time* do you mention that you are one. What else aren't you sharing?"

Karin was nailed. She had an explanation—a justified spin—but as hard as she tried to get the words out, there was no legitimate way to explain.

The truth was that Karin had been very deliberate about hiding her messy life circumstances. Even her new boss did not know what she was going through. Karin had heard enough discussion about the concept of single moms needing special accommodations to be able do their jobs. She thought, "I'm not like that. I'm a different kind of single mom. I'm an executive."

Plus, she'd been in enough closed-door discussions to know that although such circumstances shouldn't matter, they can easily lead to subtle biases that make someone else a "better fit." Karin was certain that if her secret came out, the decision makers would question her ability to travel and to work the long hours. Not to mention doubting the credibility of an HR leader who couldn't even hold her marriage together.

Suddenly Karin realized how ridiculous this all sounded, even to herself. She began checking around with some other folks on the council. One man who was gay said, "I came out to you—that took courage that you don't have. We all trusted you with some pretty big stuff, but we're starting to wonder about you. You know all about us, but we know nothing about you. We're not sure we can trust you."

Karin realized she had achieved a position but had lost the trust of her people. She had a beautiful opportunity to use her life as an example of what a single mom could achieve, to face any subtle discrimination head on and be the voice of those who did not yet have a seat at the table.

Instead she checked true courage at the door, buckled down, and protected herself, all the while creating a diversity strategy that she convinced herself (and others) was game changing.

That's not game changing. That's gaming. Imagine the impact she could have had if she had led from who she truly was.

Have you ever felt like Karin, fearful of letting others know what's really going on for fear you might be judged?

WHY YOU AND YOUR TEAM YEARN FOR AUTHENTICITY

We've never met a team that wished their manager was less authentic. It's hard to overdo this one. Authenticity also serves you. Here are a few reasons why managers and their teams yearn for authenticity.

1. The team has been screwed before.

Oh, they have stories. Trust us. We hear them. Assume somewhere along the line they've felt betrayed. Even if it's not at your company or even under your watch, once upon a time, a manager has lied to them. Guaranteed. Their guard is up. They need someone to restore their trust in authority. They need reassurance in action, not words.

They're not going to tell you the truth until they are perfectly sure you've been doing the same, over and over. Your team also desperately wants to know that the good guys can (and do) win. There's no better gift you can give your team than leading from who you are toward head-turning results.

2. You waste *your* energy.

Keeping up appearances is an energy-sucking, never-ending vacuum of misery. Trying to lead like someone else, or spin the truth, will wear you down and make you cranky. Your team would rather you show up real, and devote your energy to supporting them than to keeping up a façade. Gamers spend their time working to show up differently from who they are, to keep up a facade, and they waste precious energy that could be invested in creating break-through vision, developing people, and doing the work.

3. You waste *their* energy.

When you aren't authentic, you guide your team to behaviors that are a waste of energy. If your team senses you're playing games, they'll spend a lot of time trying to figure out the rules of that game rather than doing productive work. In fact, if you have surface success, they'll be taking notes to learn to play it too. All that façade building is contagious. It pulls hearts and minds from the important mission at hand. Your team would rather spend their energy working on the work than trying to play your game.

4. You're their lifeline.

Particularly in a big organization, the immediate manager makes all the difference. You can't outsource leadership, not even to your boss or to HR. Your people want to hear the story from you, and they want to know you don't just read talking points crafted from someone else. If they can't trust you to be genuine, where will they turn? That answer may be really dangerous.

5. They want to be like you—maybe.

Some folks on your team have serious aspirations to move up in the organization, but they don't want to lose their souls in the process. They're watching you to see how you handle the pressure. Do you stay true to who you are, or are you being groomed to be just like those above you?

6. They have important news to share.

They've got ideas and solutions, but your team wants to ensure that they'll have a receptive audience. If you're afraid to share with them, they'll be reluctant to share with you.

To be real with your team, you first have to be real with yourself. Know that you're not perfect and you have so much value to share.

FACE YOUR FEARS

There's a scene in *Harry Potter and the Chamber of Secrets* when Professor Lupin teaches the students about boggarts—shapeshifters that take on the form of whatever a person fears the most. A boggart is inside an antique, cobweb-covered cabinet that stands eight feet high. The cabinet begins to rock, and you hear a tap-tap-tapping turn into a crescendo of banging. The boggart is clearly trying to escape.

One by one, Lupin instructs the students to visualize their biggest fear—to imagine what will be coming out of that cabinet. And then he teaches them a secret.

"Luckily a very simple charm exists to repel a boggart."

It turns out you can tame your fears by making them look ridiculous.

Neville fears the intimidating Professor Snape. To conquer his fear and vanquish the boggart, Neville imagines Snape dressed as his grandmother with a big red handbag and a huge hat with a stuffed vulture on the top. Everyone laughs and—poof!—the fear vanishes.

Our biggest leadership screw-ups are fear in disguise. Fears have a powerful and dangerous habit of shape-shifting into a monster that stands in our way, blocking the behaviors we most need for success.

Karin's biggest fear when she led the diversity council was that if people knew she was a single mom, they would lose respect for her. As it turned out, that was ridiculous. Ironically, the behavior she used to protect herself, hiding that fact, was what made them lose respect.

Now, you may be wondering what fear would come out of your cabinet. Most of us have several choices.

Let's try it.

Shut your eyes. Imagine that old rickety cabinet with your boggart inside. What does it look like? Name it. Now find an image that would make it ridiculous.

When we can name our fear and see it for what it truly is—a ridiculous exaggeration of the worst-case scenario—we can stop the cycle. It's nearly impossible to be real when you're scared. To lead more authentically, get in touch with what most scares you.

TWO WORDS THAT IMMEDIATELY BUILD CREDIBILITY AND TRUST

During his teaching days, David led a team of teachers and high school students on a Rocky Mountain white-water-rafting trip. They had just finished on the water, changed into fresh clothes, and loaded up their convoy of vans to head out to the hotel.

David confidently led the line of vans out of the parking lot and onto a frontage road that ran parallel to the highway before it crossed over and merged with the highway—or so he thought.

With the other drivers in tight formation behind him, he led the team up a hill, but as he crested the hill and descended the other side, it looked like the road narrowed. He slowed a bit but kept going; they were in the mountains, after all, and roads there aren't always built perfectly.

However, as he continued down the hill, the asphalt dwindled until it was just wide enough for one vehicle before it took a sharp right turn and disappeared out of sight under the highway.

Then he saw it.

A round cornering mirror—the kind of mirror you see in grocery stores or bike paths with blind corners. The type of mirror that allows bike riders to see approaching traffic around the corner.

Yes, bikes.

He'd led his team down a bike path.

Now they were stuck—a line of vans pointed downhill on a narrow bike path. The ground on either side of the path was soft, and there was no room to turn around and no way to go forward.

Have you ever led your team down a dead end? Maybe you had a bad idea, your information was wrong, or you just plain screwed up?

If not, it's just a matter of time. As a manager, you can't live in fear of never making a mistake. Sometimes you have to take action with the best information you have and move your team forward.

If it doesn't work out, and especially if you made a true mistake, what you do next makes all the difference in whether your team will trust you in the future. What you say next will answer the most vital question they have about you: Can we really trust you? The times you screw up give you the greatest opportunities to answer this question. In these moments, you have the chance to build your credibility and your team's trust—or to go in the other direction and lose it.

On the bike path, David had to ask all the students to hike back up the hill and down the other side. Once the students were clear, he and another teacher backed each vehicle up the path, then back down the other side until they reached the parking lot where they could turn around.

Also, he had to apologize.

Your team needs to hear you say two words that immediately build credibility and trust: "I'm sorry."

Many times, managers are reluctant to apologize because they fear they'll be seen as incompetent or weak. This fear ignores one prominent fact: Your team already knows you're not perfect.

It was quite clear to everyone in those vans that David had led them down a bike path. In the same way, your team usually knows or strongly suspects when you've screwed up. It's not a secret.

When you refuse to acknowledge that you goofed up, your employees learn to emulate your behavior. They won't trust you, because they know perfection in others isn't real. In contrast, when you screw up and apologize, you actually increase your team's trust in you. They know:

- You are strong enough to do the right thing.

- You have the integrity to admit the truth even when it doesn't cast you in the best light.

- You don't consider yourself more valuable than your team.

- You're committed to solutions and the mission above appearances.

That knowledge suggests that you're reliable, credible, and can be trusted. When you make a mistake, there are just a few simple things to do:

1. Take responsibility. Admit what happened. Keep it simple. Don't make excuses, but you also don't have to beat yourself up.

2. Apologize. Use sincere, plain, straightforward language, like you would with a friend or a spouse. Never apologize like a politician.

   Do This: "I am so, so sorry. I've got to take responsibility for that." (sincere, simple)

   Don't Do This: "I regret if you felt bad about what I might have said." (indirect, political, blame-shifting)

3. Make it right. If there is something you need to correct, fix, or restore, do it. Those vans had to be backed up and turned around.

David has recalled that moment on the bike path many times through the years. When he makes a mistake, he knows that the shortest path to get things going right again is to back up the van and find the right road. When you apologize, you model accountability, you build trust, and you give everyone a chance to move forward.

When you apologize, you model accountability,
you build trust, and you give everyone a chance
to move forward.

TELL OTHERS THE TRUTH

Real is a two-way street.

Your team wants to see you for who you are. They also want to know that you're telling them the truth.

It takes real confidence to tell the truth. When you sugarcoat, it's easy to pretend that you're protecting other people, but mostly you're protecting yourself. That's not confidence, that's not humility—and it certainly won't help build relationships or achieve lasting results.

Three Rules for Speaking the Truth

Follow these three rules consistently and you're more likely to be seen as a manager who wins well.

1. Lose the Diaper Genie and be direct.

We're not fans of the sandwich feedback technique so frequently taught in management training (i.e., give positive feedback, offer your criticism, close with something positive). It's way too much for people to hear, and the positive aspects often end up feeling like BS, and all the person can hear is what's wrong.

We've called this less-than-real feedback Diaper Genie feedback ever since a blog subscriber sent Karin this note:

"I took my first real leadership position when my oldest son was still in diapers. Every time I used our Diaper Genie, I thought, this is just how feedback and bad news works. Each level takes the poop and seals it in a bag before it gets sent to the next level up. Then, that level sanitizes it some more with another layer of protection. By the time it gets to the top, it smells pretty benign."

You're much better off starting from a place of genuine caring and being direct. We offer a technique at the end of this chapter that will help.

2. Stop spinning.

Have you ever sat in a manager meeting with your peers going around and around asking, "How do we explain this to our employees in a way they can hear, understand, and feel good about?" How you position a difficult message matters—a lot.

And yet, if you find yourself in meeting after meeting working to wordsmith your communication to better "position" what is happening, we encourage you to ask one question: "What if you told your employees the truth?"

- Overtime is too high; we must increase productivity.

- The stock price is stagnant; we will all benefit from better financials.

- We need to ensure that everyone is contributing.

- This new automation will be more efficient.

People want the truth. Not spin. Most people will respect you far more for being real than for any elegant positioning you can concoct.

When people feel respected, they will respond.

When people feel respected, they will join.

When people feel respected, they will try.

At the same time, unfiltered truth shared in an uncaring way creates unproductive havoc. Start with the truth and then consider:

- What are the best and worst parts of this situation?

- Who will this impact in what ways?

- What questions will be most relevant to whom?

- What additional information should I have available?

- What other questions will they ask?

We have never regretted erring on the side of the truth even when it was scary. Even if the awkward truth creates short-term anxiety, when you communicate well, the credibility you establish is worth the risk.

3. Be Open to the truths of others.

Be real with your team and let them be real with you. If you're going to change the game, you'll need a big dose of real.

It may not seem like it at the time, but we've both found that most folks do appreciate the truth, even when it's hard to hear. Your employees will be better off in the long run if you're honest and don't let a bad situation linger too long.

YOUR WINNING WELL ACTION PLAN

1. What would be different if you were more real with your team?

2. What fear would come out of your leadership cabinet? Name it. How can you follow Professor Lupin's example and see that the fear is ridiculous?

3. Is there a place where you have let your people down? Hurt them? Broken a commitment? If so, when and how can you apologize to restore your credibility?

4. Write down and revisit your leadership credo. Writing down your "This is what I believe" statement is a good way to keep yourself in check. We try to do this after each assignment. Take some time every year, or after each assignment, to write down what you believe, and score yourself from time to time. The exercise can be truly humbling. For a step-by-step guide to building your leadership credo, visit our website, www. WinningWellBook.com.

It's Time to Win Well

You've received many tools to help you win well and sustain excellent results over time. However, in our experience there are common roadblocks that will arise and have the potential to keep you from using what you've learned. Many of these obstacles include the people around you: your boss and your employees. In this section we discuss some of the most common scenarios you'll encounter and give you the tools to win well through all of them. We close with solutions to work with the most troublesome obstacle you may ever encounter: yourself.

CHAPTER 22

What If My Boss Doesn't Want to Win and Doesn't Care About Their Soul— or Mine?

"No man chooses evil because it is evil; he only mistakes it for happiness, the good he seeks."

—MARY WOLLSTONECRAFT

You're working hard to be a manager who wins well, but what if your boss is more of a User, Gamer, or Pleaser? How can you still win well?

• • •

Jamie shut the door and began the emergency meeting. What he had to say wasn't easy, but he knew his people could handle it. That's why they "get paid the big bucks." He minced no words. Stock prices, competitive pressures, time to get it together. *Now.* The intimidation factor was high. His face red and blotchy, he barked, "Fix it fast or else!"

He would *never* speak this way to the front line. He's an inspiring communicator, and his people love him. He trusted his leaders would translate the message in a meaningful way.

Grace, the new vice president, left Jamie's meeting a bit shaken but clear on the message. She called an emergency huddle with her direct reports. They were in the midst of executing plans to address key issues, but she worried it wouldn't be fast enough. She needed to show progress *right away*. She took Jamie's remarks to heart and was pretty sure her job was on the line.

She didn't usually rely on fear and intimidation. Most of the time she was a role model of Winning Well behaviors, but she was still learning the culture and figured that people were accustomed to this. Plus, her team was full of seasoned leaders who understood the pressure. She would *never* speak that way to the front line, but she trusted that her team would know how to communicate the message in a meaningful way.

Grace's technical manager, Bill, left their meeting a bit shocked. "Wow," he thought. "Grace has never acted this way before. She doesn't even seem to want our input. She just told us what to do. Something must be really wrong. If this is what she's telling us, I wonder what she's holding back."

Bill was concerned that his team of operations supervisors wouldn't buy into her plan. After all, it had been a crazy couple of months, and they were all about to tip over from exhaustion. Plus, he knew the decision was shortsighted, would reduce quality, and would cause rework down the line.

Clearly, though, the situation was serious, so he decided to just be a good soldier and salute. He was behind on his mortgage, and his daughter was headed to college. This was no time to stand out as a naysayer.

Bill called a meeting of his operations supervisors and laid it all on the line. He needed to get their attention, so he figured a little bit of intimidation couldn't hurt. Plus, he knew he was on the short list for a transfer to another department. He wouldn't have to deal with the downstream effect.

So Bill told his supervisors, "I want you to fix this, by whatever means necessary. If anyone complains, write them up for insubordination." Bill knew he was being a bit rough. He would *never* talk that way to the technicians. But he had good supervisors who he trusted would buffer the message.

Imagine you report to Bill? What are the chances you would use Winning Well behaviors as you talk to the technicians?

INTIMIDATION SNOWBALLS

Be careful. Gamer, User, and Pleaser characteristics are contagious. Don't let the bad behaviors rub off.

You can learn as much from a bad boss
as a good one.

First, pay close attention to how the stress impacts you, your people, and your family. Find folks who will tell you the truth. Be sure you're staying true to your leadership philosophy.

Find ways to ground yourself: think of a lightning rod. It absorbs the energy from the lightning and disburses it into the ground without allowing it to damage the building. Exercise, mediation, and prayer are all good options to ground you. Remember that you know how to win well, and your boss is just one transient person in your life. This season will end, but you will live with who you are becoming forever. Once you ground yourself and regain your bearing, consciously choose how you will interact with your people. Even in moments of high stress, you do have a choice. Choose based on your values, on confidence paired with humility, and with a focus on relationships and results.

Second, keep in mind that you can learn as much from a bad boss as a good one. Pay close attention to the impact your boss's behaviors have on you and your teammates. Keep a journal or make a running list. Commit to never being that person.

If any of the managers in the above example had had enough

confidence and humility to ask a few strategic questions or taken some time to discuss the best way to solve the problem by focusing on results and relationships, they would have likely come up with a more effective solution.

By shutting up and protecting themselves, they sold their souls and made matters worse.

HAVE A CONVERSATION

Karin recalls a time not too long ago when she felt her own soul slipping way. It had been a tough couple of weeks. The cocktail of challenges had impacted her team's normally high performance. They needed strong results immediately. She didn't realize how much her stress showed on the outside until a trusted manager on her team called her and said bluntly, "You're changing."

The words stung with fierce truth. He was right. On the inside, she was worried about their mission, their cause, and their careers. But on the outside she was acting more like a User. She was showing up like the boss she'd refused to become. Her passion to protect her team had taken on an ironic intensity. Her supportive style morphed into frantic control. She invited herself to line-level conference calls and required more rehearsals before executive presentations. Instead of trusting her competent team, she scrutinized every page of every PowerPoint deck.

Her efforts to protect her team from stress had backfired.

The words still echoed from the first conversation when her phone rang again. Another one of her managers was calling. At that moment, Karin realized that the two managers had talked before and coordinated the conversation. The second manager said, "Your style works. Stay the course. We believe in you, in us, and the mission. Every one of us has your back. Just tell us what you need."

David has heard those words, too, in very similar circumstances. Kevin, a trusted colleague and one of his direct reports, said, "You're not David anymore. What's going on? How can we help?" Sometimes bosses need to see themselves as you see them. When you hold this kind of conversation from a place of support and compassion, it's a heck of a lot more productive than being ticked off at your boss and talking behind her back.

We were the ones who needed reminding of what Winning Well looks like. Our teams reminded us that:

- We were not alone.

- Showing up tough is weak.

- Leaders serve their people when they receive truth from them.

- Great teams hold their managers accountable.

- They wanted to know the truth.

- Great leaders tell the truth.

- Courage means staying true to your style.

Over the years, we've had employees tell us how we've hurt their feelings, overlooked their efforts, embarrassed them, or overreacted. Every one of those conversations has helped the team to be stronger and helped us to be more effective.

Sometimes the best way to win well is to help your boss see the impact of his behavior on the results and people.

There are also more lighthearted ways to approach such situations.

One vice president we know had such highs and lows that her team gave her two nearly matching Barbie dolls for her desk. The first was immaculately dressed in typical Barbie fashion: matching shirt, shoes, and pearls. The other doll had felt-tip marker on her face that made her look evil, and hair that looked liked it had been eaten by a cat.

They chose a "good Barbie day" to approach her with their plan. Their request was that she put out the doll that best portrayed her mood as a warning sign. Her team then knew if evil Barbie was lurking, they needed to lie low. She accepted the gift with a smile and used the dolls as requested to lighten the mood. She even became comfortable when one of them would go to her shelf and switch the dolls to tell her the team was having a rough time with her.

Despite an occasional, frustration-induced mood swing, she

was a brilliant, inspiring, deeply devoted leader. Everyone who worked for her grew under her care. If the team had stopped caring because of her outbursts, they would have missed all she would teach them about Winning Well.

Chances are that if your boss isn't Winning Well, he doesn't feel particularly good about it. If everybody's frustrated, it's likely your boss is too. Messy relationships are always a two-way street. Be sure you do everything you can to work on the relationship.

Conversation Starters

Here are some questions you can ask your boss to get a conversation started.

1. What specifically can I do to better support our team's mission?

2. What do your peers say about me?

3. Whom should I be working with more closely?

4. What could I be doing to make your job easier?

5. To what do you attribute your own career success? How can I be more effective in that arena?

6. Which parts of my style concern you the most?

7. Specifically what do I need to work on to be ready for _____ (insert here the job or assignment you are most interested in)?

MANAGING UP WITH CONFIDENT HUMILITY

Confidence and humility are cornerstones of Winning Well. They're also vital in maintaining an effective relationship with your boss. Remember some of the confidence-leveraging behaviors: know, own, and use your strengths; stand up for what matters; and speak the truth. Be brave enough to have and share your opinions, even if they differ from those of your boss.

Of course, every boss is different. Understand and play to her style. If you struggle with persuading your boss, try the following tips:

1. Don't confront her in front of your peers, her peers, your team.

Have the conversation privately. Let your passion inspire your argument, but don't emote. Stay calm. Appeal to his heart and mind, but don't wear your heart on your sleeve. It might help to tell a story, but think it through first. Overly emotional appeals will weaken your argument.

2. Do your homework.

What are her goals? What keeps *her* boss awake at night? Put your concern in terms that are important to her. Prepare for questions. Do the math. Do more math. Do the math her way. Poke holes. If she doesn't like math, collect stories. Do more math, just in case.

Yesenia managed a group of insurance company accountants. Her group had low morale because of a problem they'd uncovered but couldn't solve. The customer service department was taking shortcuts that cost the company $3 million annually. The accountants had tried to talk to the customer service department without success. Yesenia approached the CEO to discuss the problem. She didn't lead with, "My group has a morale problem." She started with, "My group has discovered a way we can save $3 million annually. It will take some coordination with another department. Would you like to hear more?" Of course the CEO took the time to listen—because Yesenia had done her homework and shared the issue in terms that mattered to her boss.

3. Share your concern frankly.

Speak your truth. Share why you are concerned for the business. Have several supporting points. Listen carefully. Your boss has broader perspective and more context. Learn as much as you can. Hear him out completely and suspend judgment. Listen some more.

Appreciate his point of view. He's likely not a jerk. He has pressures too. Understand them. Learn all you can. Consider, deeply.

If you're still convinced, bring on the data. Build graphs. Show correlations. Draw pictures. Find stories. Benchmark with the best. Engage your support team. For us, this usually means the finance person. She's fantastic. Yours can be too. These folks are usually reasonable and thoughtful, and can help you clarify and support your position. Convince others to care about your point of view. Get a light murmur of whispers started to support your cause in other people's words.

Of course, the other side of the side of the confidence-humility spectrum is humility: Know your vulnerabilities, admit mistakes, and invite challengers. As in all relationships, humility is vital when you work to improve your relationship with your boss.

Managing Up When Things Go Wrong

Perhaps the most important time to stay humble is when you've screwed up. The biggest mistake you can make with bad news is to wait too long. Your boss would rather know what's going on, even if you don't need his help. We recommend using our DARN method to guide your approach.

D—Disclose (explain the situation and root cause)

"I've had a bad day. We have a bit of a situation I need to fill you in on." _____ happened and now we have _____. When I dug in deeper I learned it was caused by _____." (Identify a behavior or situation, not a person.)

A—Accountability (don't be a blamer)

"I accept full responsibility. Here's how I can prevent this next time _____."

R—Response (share your solution)

"Here's what I've already done _____." (It's important to have something to say here.)

N—Next Steps (share your plan and what you need)

"Here's what I'm going to do next_____. I could use your help with _____." (If needed.)

YOUR WINNING WELL ACTION PLAN

1. Think of the worst boss you've ever had. How could you have used some of these Winning Well approaches? What might have happened differently if you had used these techniques?

2. Do you ever succumb to trickle-down intimidation? What could you do to wash your hands to get back to Winning Well?

3. Think of a situation where you really want to persuade someone to see your point of view. Plan your conversation using the confidence-humility persuasion tips.

4. Download our Building a Better Relationship with Your Boss Assessment from www.WinningWellBook.com. Complete the assessment and ask one of your direct reports to complete it. Use it as a basis for conversation on how to make your relationship more productive. Once you've had some practice, see if your boss would be willing to complete the exercise with you and use it to improve that relationship as well.

CHAPTER 23

What If My Team Doesn't Want to Win?

"Being defeated is often a temporary condition.
Giving up is what makes it permanent."

—MARILYN VOS SAVANT

When you have a clear picture of where you want to go but your team won't come along as quickly as you want, it can feel like you're trying to tow a car out of mud. On a recent trip to the mountains, one of David's daughter's friends, Geoff, drove his car into a ditch. There was nearly two feet of snow on top of slick mud, and Geoff slid off the road just a few hundred yards from the cabin where David was staying. As he tried to back out, his wheels sank. It was time for a tow.

Fortunately, Geoff had a tow cable and David's SUV has low-ratio four-wheel drive. They secured the cable to both vehicles, and Geoff asked what would happen next. He had never been on either end of a tow before, so they discussed why the cable was hooked to the cars' frames, what direction they would go, and how to gradually build momentum. They also talked about how failure to do these things would end up damaging one or both of their vehicles.

Towing and management have some things in common. When you sense that your team doesn't want to win or follow your lead, it can feel just like you're stuck in the mud, spinning your wheels. There are several ways you can restore momentum when your people don't seem to care.

A good tow depends on a solid connection between the two vehicles. For example, don't hook your tow cable to the bumper of either vehicle. This is a weak connection. In fact, you can watch hours of videos online where people rip the bumper right off of a friend's car. They didn't attach their cable to the car's frame, and when they pulled, they tore the car apart.

Just as you want to connect a tow cable to a car's frame, as a manager, your influence depends on the strength of your connection to your people. Share the meaning and purpose behind the work. Know what your people value, and connect those values to their daily tasks.

The most meaningful connections you make are with shared values and clear reasons why activities must happen. Without these connections, you've probably asked your team to do something that makes no sense to them (with little chance of success).

Your influence depends on the strength of your connection to your people.

You also strengthen your connection to your people when you get their input (see Chapter 6). Ask what they think the team is capable of, why they do what they do, and how they would improve the results they produce.

When you tow, you don't want to pull the car sideways or you could rip off a tire or an entire axle. Instead, start by pulling the vehicle in the direction it was going or else directly opposite that direction. This minimizes stress on the car and gets the wheels rolling.

Similarly with your team, you have to know their current capacity, training, and priorities. If you ask something of them that they don't know how to do, or that their current workload can't accommodate, or something that is in conflict with their current priorities, you'll end up frustrated.

We've worked with many User managers who respond to this scenario by pulling harder (they yell, belittle their people, and get upset). This is the equivalent of pulling at the wrong angle and tearing the axle off the car. At best, your people lose respect for you. At worse, they rebel, quit, or sabotage.

When you need to get your team going a different direction, start by examining the capacity, training, and priorities. What can you remove from their plate? What training can you get for them? How can you help reprioritize and gradually get them rolling in the new direction?

Don't slam on the accelerator. When David pulled Geoff out of the ditch, the dirt road was very muddy. If he had accelerated too quickly, his tires would have spun and dug into the mud, trapping both of them.

Had the road been dry and he had gone too fast, he would have ripped something off one vehicle or else snapped the tow cable. As a manager, you have a clear picture of where you're going and what needs to happen to get there. It's obvious to you.

But what's obvious to you won't be obvious to your people without significant communication. We've worked with countless numbers of frustrated managers who told their team about a change in procedure once, six months ago, and are now angry that their team isn't implementing the change.

To pull gently and build momentum, you've got to frequently communicate what's happening, why it's happening, and the specific tasks each person is responsible for, and then check for understanding. At the end of discussions, ask team members to share what they understand the expectations to be.

Slow down just a little bit, and help your people build momentum in the new direction.

LOST FAITH

The next area to address in order to restore momentum is your team's beliefs. Remember, you give your team a chance to follow you when you clearly connect their work to meaning, purpose, and shared values. Ensure that they have the capacity to do what's necessary and communicate well.

But what if you've done all of that, and they're still slowly sinking deeper into the mud? When inertia like that sets in, there's almost always a breakdown in belief at some level. When teams stop believing they stop doing. If your team has lost that magic feeling, look for signs of lost believing.

1. They stop believing in you.

This can take a variety of forms, but it almost always comes down to a matter of trust. They no longer believe you have their backs. Or they've stopped believing you have the guts to speak the truth, up, down, or sideways. Or perhaps they don't believe your guidance is sound.

This is a hard one to fix, and you won't be successful until you address the real issue. Look for ways to open the conversation one on one to get to the root cause. Know that your words will go only so far. Your team will scrutinize every behavior for signs of what to really believe.

2. They stop believing in the organization.

The trust in you may run deep, but if the team has started to question the ethics or the future of the organization, they may be distracted and lose steam. They're watching you for clues—they won't believe if you don't believe, so be sure to check your attitudes, beliefs, and behaviors.

If you suspect that the team has concerns in this arena, give them an opportunity to express and discuss their concerns. It's likely that the story they're telling themselves is much worse than the truth.

3. They stop believing in the cause.

People are motivated by "why" far more than "how." Ensure that your staff understands the greater good and how they fit in. It's a good time to ensure that you have a strong team vision and that each person knows where and why she fits in.

4. They stop believing in one another.

No employee-engagement strategy is going to work if your employees don't trust and believe in one another. Take a close look at what you're doing to practice accountability, remove obstacles, and encourage teamwork.

5. They stop believing in themselves.

You can have a clear role and vision, and a group that gets along like peanut butter and jelly, but if the individuals on the team lack confidence in their ability to execute, they won't succeed. It's good to periodically gauge confidence levels at an individual and a team level. If they think your goal is impossible, they'll talk themselves out of trying.

6. They stop believing they can make a difference.

Perhaps they've worked on a big project only to see a change in direction make their work obsolete. Or perhaps the downstream processes are so screwed up that any work they do is inadvertently sabotaged by later incompetence. If people don't think their work really matters, they stop doing work that really matters.

Fix these issues and look for ways to restore value to their work. You may need to enlist help higher up the organization chart.

INDIVIDUAL SOUL SUCKERS

Another area to examine when your people are stuck and don't want to win is the individual.

Karin's heart sank as she heard all that Kathy had done attempting to fix the situation. Actually, despite Kathy's concern, the project was progressing remarkably. Kathy and her team had come so far in such a short time: a clear vision for the year, a strong action plan on the biggest goal, a shared leadership model for execution, and Kathy had stepped up to lead her peers in coordinating the action plan.

When they presented the plan to the CEO the month before, he remarked that the plan was "gold." All they needed now was execution.

Kathy had tasted the beautiful cocktail of pressure coupled with opportunity and was ready to win well, but her call to Karin wasn't about all that. She was stuck.

"Everyone's on board. But one of my peers hates it."

She went through everything she had tried to get him engaged. Connection. Listening. Disclosure. More listening. Questions. Vulnerability. Inclusion. Sharing Credit.

Nothing worked and she concluded, "This means I'm failing as a leader."

How many times have you drawn that same conclusion? Yes, start with humility and do everything you can, but sometimes it's not about you. Ironically, if you think it's always about you, that's not humility.

Careful to be sure Karin hadn't missed anything, she asked Kathy to repeat exactly what she'd said. This time she added, "I know I'm not always like this, but this time, I'm sure. I was really nice. I promise."

This could be part of the issue. People remember your past behavior even as you try to grow. Kathy had been pretty rough in the past, and it's possible the guy was bracing himself for the other shoe to drop.

Kathy shared the connection she'd made with the other team members. The engagement. The helping people get past "I'm not sure." She had done well.

Then Karin wondered, "Yikes, maybe I'm the one failing." She was out of provocative questions, and even worse, advice. She asked the one remaining question:

"Can you succeed without him?"

"Yes," Kathy replied, "But it won't be as much fun." That's the spirit. Kathy had the big picture.

Karin continued, "I understand. Does the business need this? Is everyone else all in?"

"Yes. Yes. Yes." Kathy said.

Karin concluded, "Do everything you can to try to get him on board. Stay confident in your vision, humble in your approach. But at the end of the day, move the project forward, and be sure to keep your boss in the loop."

Sometimes when a team sinks, it's because one or two employees act as big, heavy anchors pulling everyone down deeper into the muck. When you let this soul-sucking behavior continue, it reduces your credibility, causes your best performers to bolt, and leaves the rest of the employees wondering why they bother. High performers hate watching their saboteur teammates pour water in the mud pit. If you've tried the techniques we've talked about in previous chapters and they're still sloshing around like pigs in mud, with no intention of improving, make the tough call and let them go (with compassion; see Chapter 11).

YOUR WINNING WELL ACTION PLAN

1. Do you still believe that your team can win? If the answer to this is "No," see Chapter 24.

2. Is the entire group struggling, or are one or two troublemakers slowing momentum?

3. If the entire team is stuck, is there a lack of connection? Are you pulling in a different direction than they're able to go? Are you moving too fast? Or is there a place where they lack belief? How can you address the real issue and restore their momentum?

4. If the issue is one or two troublemakers, what keeps you from addressing them directly?

5. How can you overcome this resistance and help your team move forward?

6. Ask yourself some questions based on Section 3:

- Do I *see* them for who they are?
- Do I *trust* them?
- Am I *supporting* them?
- Am I *connecting* with them?
- Am I *hearing* what they are telling me?
- Am *including* them?
- Are we *succeeding*?
- Am I *recognizing* their contributions?
- Are we *having fun*?
- Am I *real* with them?

CHAPTER 24

How to Inspire and Motivate Yourself

"Winning isn't getting ahead of others,
it's getting ahead of yourself."
—ROGER STAUBACH

You cannot hope to take your people someplace you cannot go yourself. This becomes more difficult when you don't have a Winning Well manager yourself. Fortunately, you can inspire and motivate yourself when you take responsibility for yourself first, empower yourself with a simple question, find confidence even when you don't feel it, and learn how to thrive even in a negative workplace.

We hope that as you've read *Winning Well* you've found wisdom that smacks you right between the eyes. The tools, tips, and tactics you've received have the power to transform your work and your life, but there is a sneaky trap that can prevent you from accruing those benefits. It's a seductive trap, and its siren song has snared many well-intentioned managers.

We know because we've both been seduced by its powerful grasp.

The trap is problematic because it feels so good, but it's 100 percent effective at preventing your growth as a manager. We call this pernicious threat evangelist syndrome.

Here's how it works: You read a book and realize just how meaningful the information is, and then, just when you might start to benefit from it, the thought occurs to you, "So and so really needs this." Evangelist syndrome can take different forms:

1. "My boss needs to read this book right away."

2. "I just wish my manager was here."

3. "My colleague needs this list."

4. "I need to share this content with my team."

Evangelist syndrome is the tendency we have when we come across something meaningful to immediately apply it to others. If you're a manager committed to the growth of your employees, this tendency can feel very altruistic. After all, you're looking out for their interests and helping their professional development, right? If managers frustrate you, it's very easy to wish those leaders would practice what you just discovered. Either way, this seductive trap keeps you from the most important work: applying your learning to you.

Before you get everyone in your life a copy of this book, take a moment and ask yourself:

1. Is this information I have mastered in my own management practices?

2. Can the person I want to share with look to me as an example?

3. Have I committed to learning and applying the information in my life?

If the answer to any of these questions is "No," then start with you. Make the commitment to master the principles, practices, and tips you've come across. Apply them to your own life first. Then invite others to join you on the journey. Instead of starting with,

"My boss is a jerk, and she really needs to read this," start with, "How can this help me to be the leader I want my boss to be?" Once you've made that commitment, then buy as many copies as your mail carrier can hold.

THREE WORDS THAT WILL TRANSFORM YOUR LIFE AND LEADERSHIP

A few months ago Karin received this email from Jason, a reader of her blog:

> *Would you be up to offer a little free advice to a beat-down manager? I have been in some type of leadership position for over a decade now. Two years ago I took over as manager of the noted "most challenging group" in our company. A slight understatement, but I was up for the challenge.*
>
> *A few months ago, in discussions with my director he informed me that I needed to win my team over and that I did not have their respect. I have never had anyone tell me anything like that with either of the two previous teams that I oversaw. Dazed and confused I moved forward.*
>
> *I have worked beside them and did the same jobs that they were doing, brought them breakfast or donuts when I held early morning meetings. Taken some of them to lunch at local steakhouses when the work that I needed them to do was tedious, dirty and nasty. Championed their need for better tools and equipment and got it. I have stood before them and asked them to tell me what they needed me to do to work better for them and make their work lives better—very few responses but at least a couple of them offered.*
>
> *Today I was lambasted by my director because of one individual who easily gets his feelings hurt when he is required to do more than he believes he should be doing. The epitome of, "I'll do what I want to." This has happened on three different occasions. Each time I have tried a new approach, eased into conversations with this individual, and now have all but stopped trying to work with him. I only get in trouble when I do.*

So, tell me how you would proceed. I am at my wits' end. I am giving up. It became painfully obvious to me when I began this email seeking advice from an unfamiliar, outside source.

By now you're a Winning Well expert, with tools to uncover the root cause of the situation and make it better. What would you do next if you were Jason's coach?

We imagine you'd want to ask some great questions and use a sprinkling of tools from Sections 2 and 3, and then jump to Chapter 23 and help him manage his boss better too. It's easier when you look at someone else's problem, isn't it?

It happens to all of us. We all have times in our careers where we feel stuck, lack confidence, or wonder why no one sees things our way.

If you've ever felt even a third of what Jason's feeling, it's easy to think, "Maybe I should just give up."

When it gets that bad, we encourage you to start with three words: "How can I . . . ?"

With those three words you:

- Return focus to your own power and ability to act
- Tap into the energy of your prefrontal cortex, the part of your brain that problem solves and plans
- Vastly increase the odds of finding a solution

Take responsibility and ownership for the one thing you can control: yourself. Let's try some "How can I . . ." questions with Jason's situation.

- How can I better understand this employee's resistance?
- How can I find a better fit for this employee?
- How can I get more input and feedback from my team?
- How can I set clearer expectations?
- How can I build better understanding with my boss?

Or maybe even:

• How can I find a job that doesn't make me so frustrated?

When you ask, "How can I . . . ?" you might honestly respond with, "I don't know." That's okay. Use the follow-up question we discussed earlier: "What might I do if I did know?"

Now watch what happens. It's amazing how you can generate ideas when you give yourself permission. Sometimes you'll realize that you don't have the information you need in order to craft solutions. Then the question becomes, "How can I get the information I need?"

HOW TO LEAD WHEN YOU LACK CONFIDENCE

Throughout this book we've talked consistently about the importance of confidence and humility, results and relationships. So many of the managers we work with tell us the hardest part to master is confidence.

Even those highly successful managers who appear to be Winning Well and making a difference will often take us aside and admit that they sometimes feel like a fake.

They feel as if their success rests on a knife's edge: One false move, one tiny mistake, and everyone would know they were nothing but a well-spoken fraud.

This is what's known as imposter syndrome.

Impostor syndrome describes that feeling of strong self-doubt that you're a fake, that your success is due more to luck or your ability to fool people than it is due to your work, and it often comes along with the fear of being found out.

If you let it, impostor syndrome will tie you in knots, ruin your confidence, and undermine your ability to lead your people and achieve your goals—not to mention screw up your life in many other ways.

We know. We've been there too.

At earlier times in our lives, we each felt as if we didn't belong in that boardroom, didn't think that others would take us seriously, or that we weren't as smart, as proficient, as musical, or as experienced as we needed to be compared to the group we were working with.

The brutal truth is that you can't be the manager you need to be when you're tied up in knots like that. You'll try to overcompensate, or you'll stay silent when you should speak. Either one will kill your credibility and end your influence. There are several tools you can use to overcome this self-sabotage. Here are just a few:

1. Honor your past and your present.

One of David's mentors said, "It's a good thing to remember where you come from, but it's a foolish thing to think you're still there."

His point is that your experiences in childhood and earlier life can serve you, help you make good decisions, give you an appreciation for people from all walks of life, and keep you from being judgmental. It would be foolish to leave that treasure behind. But, it would be equally foolhardy not to acknowledge today's circumstances. That's intellectually dishonest and dishonors the people who have put their trust in you today.

2. Remember that, "You're always too something for someone."

These wise words come from 1999 world champion of public speaking and motivational speaker Craig Valentine. "You're always too something for someone" gets at the absurdity of it all because once you start looking for inadequacy, you'll always find a reason you don't belong.

3. Laugh at your doubts.

When David writes and self-doubt begins to wrap him in its constricting coils, telling him he can't write anything unless it's absolutely perfect, he can almost hug that little voice, laugh at it, and say, "Ahhh, there you are again, aren't you cute?" It's hard to be critical when you're adorable.

4. Examine it before you swallow it.

Sometimes your doubts might have something important to tell you. Maybe there is a new skill you need to learn or a true mistake you can avoid. How can you tell the difference between legitimate doubt and useless insecurity?

Picture someone tossing you an apple. You don't catch the apple with your teeth, immediately chew it, and swallow it. You catch it in your hand; then you might inspect the apple and decide if you want to eat it. Treat doubts and criticisms like the apple. Don't automatically swallow them. Ask yourself if there is something of value for you here. Create space for curiosity. See what happens. You get to choose whether you take a bite from the apple and internalize the concern or toss it away.

If you're still unsure, this is a great place for a mentor or coach to assist you.

5. Use your people.

One of the most effective tools for dealing with impostor syndrome is simply to focus on the team you serve. They don't really care where you came from, how you got here, whether you have a big house, small car, good hair, bad hair, or anything else. What they do care about is how you can help them succeed today. It's nearly impossible to trip over your own insecurities when you focus on serving others. This is the reason volunteering is such a powerful experience and why you hear volunteers say they received so much more than they gave.

WINNING WELL IN A
NEGATIVE WORKPLACE

Karin's German father-in-law would call trying to fix a negative workplace, "Furzen gegen den Donner." In English, that's "farting against thunder." That's the situation where Janet, a financial services manager, found herself.

Janet's supervisory situation seemed pretty futile: little to no recognition, development, or teamwork combined with long hours, limited resources, lots of finger-pointing, and the uncertainty of a new acquisition and consolidation.

When Janet tried to get a list of the company values, no one seemed to know where to find them. The veterans knew they existed somewhere. They were as hard to find as the vacation policy no one took seriously. Leaders were fleeing this negative workplace every day. And yet Janet had made a deliberate decision to stay and was pulling people together to improve the situation.

Karin asked her why.

"I used to feel like I needed to get out of here, but now I'm so excited to be part of the solution. It is fulfilling to see progress. I know I may lose my job in a year or so, but for now this feels like important work."

Important work, indeed. Janet was doing her best to be a role model of Winning Well, even in less-than-ideal circumstances. It's far easier to run away, but the world needs people who dive deeper to change a negative workplace. Here are some tips that can help.

1. Make a list of what you like most about your job. Share it with others. Ask them what they like most about their jobs.

2. Ask people why they work. In a negative environment, the answer may seem obvious—"For the paycheck, stupid"—but take it a step further. Do they work to support their sick mom? To pay back student loans? To save for their children's education? Because they enjoy helping customers? Reconnecting to the purpose of work can help make the smaller annoyances less frustrating.

3. Call out negativity. When you see negative thinking or actions, talk to the person privately to call it out, particularly if other leaders are involved. When negative attitudes and talk are all around, it's tempting to ignore it. Raise the bar and change the conversation.

4. Rise above the drama. Refuse to get sucked into the rumors and gossip. Respond to your team's concerns with transparency and candor. Be the one who people know they can trust for a straight answer.

5. Find kindred spirits. Not everyone is negative, although it can feel that way at times. Look around and find other folks

trying to change the scene for the better. There is strength in numbers. Look outside your organization as well.

6. Create an "envelope of excellence" or cultural oasis. It's easy to feel overwhelmed trying to fix the overall culture. Start with your own team and do what you can to make it feel better to come to work.

7. Find reasons to celebrate. With all the negativity, it's easy to overlook the good. Go out of your way to recognize and celebrate small wins. Substitute weak phrases like "No problem" with more enthusiastic words like "I'd be happy to."

8. See barriers as a challenge. Encourage your team to embrace the problems they see as opportunities and challenges to learn and grow. Recap learning along the way to help them feel a sense of positive momentum even during the most challenging times.

9. Laugh more. Karin had one colleague who would respond to the company's most ridiculous political nonsense by reminding the team, "It's all comedy." Step back and recognize how ridiculous some behavior is. You'll create a healthy distance from which to respond more appropriately.

10. Hold deeper developmental conversations. In periods of uncertainty, people yearn for a sense of control and connection. Take your developmental conversations to the next level. Ask your team and your peers about their hopes and dreams, what motivates them, and what scares them. Show up as a real human being caring about other real human beings.

YOUR WINNING WELL ACTION PLAN

1. What do you like most about your job?

2. What about your job frustrates you? What are three "How can I . . . ?" questions you can ask yourself to take responsibility and improve your situation? Ask them and write down your answers.

3. What are you doing to take care of yourself? What one thing could you add to your daily routine that would make you feel healthier?

4. How can you create an envelope of excellence for you and your people regardless of what's happening in the rest of your organization?

5. Are you feeling particularly disgruntled, trapped, in conflict with yourself, or underutilized? If so, how can you work to improve your situation either within your current organization or another one?

CHAPTER 25

Your Winning Well Legacy

*"Carve your name on hearts, not tombstones.
A legacy is etched into the minds of others and
the stories they share about you."*

—SHANNON L. ALDER

ow do you know that you're Winning Well? Do you make an impact in your work and your life? Are you leaving a legacy for your employees and family? How will you be remembered?

These are tough questions to answer. First, we'll start with where not to look.

• • •

Karin recently met Julie, a successful entrepreneur, at a large national conference. Julie confided, "I just love coming to this conference, but I had to stop coming for a while."

Karin was sure Julie was going to tell her about finances, a booked business calendar, or kids' soccer schedules. Instead, Julie said:

"Don't get me wrong. The convention has always been amazing. The trouble is, I would be totally happy before I came. I loved my life. I had a strong business that I juggled well with the priority of raising my children. But then I would come to the conference and see how much everyone else was doing to build their career, and I would get depressed thinking of all the things I *should* be doing. For a while it was just easier to stay away."

"How do you feel about your choices now?" Karin asked.

Julie lit up. "Fantastic. My kids are all good human beings doing well in the world. I was able to involve them in some of my travel as I built the business, and also to be around. I built a strong foundation for my career, and now that the kids are older, I make more discretionary money that we use for big family vacations with our grown kids. They want to hang out with us. I feel really good about my choices. I have no regrets."

They talked about motherhood and values, raising children deliberately, and saving money for vacations. Karin couldn't resist. "You might really enjoy my ebook on developing leadership in kids. It's free. Want me to send you a copy?

"No way!" Julie replied.

Now Karin was a bit puzzled.

Then Julie said matter-of-factly, "Every time I read a book like that, I feel I should have written it, and it makes me sad."

"Shoulds" are powerful and dangerous. "Should haves" are a soul-sucking waste of time. Be sure your "shoulds" are your own. If they won't shut up, then turn your "shoulds" into concrete plans, but don't let them judge you and make you sad.

HOW WINNING WELL MANAGERS MEASURE SUCCESS

How can you be sure your day-to-day activities are making a long-term impact? This can be a challenging question to answer. Day by day, time seems to move slowly, and you may wonder whether you're making a difference.

If you're a parent, you know that one day you struggle to get your child to eat or clean up his room and then, before you can turn around, he's grown up and left home. If you garden, you're familiar with this same movement of time. One day you plant seeds, then you wait and it seems like nothing happens. Many days later, the seeds sprout. Some days it feels like the weeds will completely take over. On any one day, you hardly see any growth at all, and yet, by the end of the summer, you've got squash, tomatoes, and cucumbers ready to eat.

Your work as a manager follows the same rhythms of life. Each day doesn't seem to make a huge difference, but before you know it, those days have added up to weeks, months, and even years or decades you've spent with people.

As you assess your impact, we invite you to revisit the Winning Well model. First start with your values and how you feel on the inside—how's your confidence-humility balance?

Are you able to manage your team according to the values you hold most deeply? Do you stand up for what you believe and speak the truth, even when it's hard?

How do you feel on the humility front? Do you have a realistic view of where you need to improve? Do you surround yourself with people who will tell you the truth? Are you listening well? The truth is, you can't win well on the outside if you're not Winning Well on the inside.

You can't win well on the outside if you're not Winning Well on the inside.

On the people front, do you build healthy relationships, investing in people and seeing people grow?

At the end of every day, can you look back and find at least one place you invested in another person? Did you encourage someone? Did you teach her? Did you empower her and see her get stronger as a result? Did you resolve a conflict? Did you hold someone accountable?

Are the employees you work with better because of their time with you? That's a simple but powerful test of your leadership, and it's all about the health of your relationships.

The next benchmark is results. At the end of every day, can you look back and find at least one place or that one most important thing that contributes to the results you're responsible for achieving?

You won't see a finished product every day, any more than you'll see your children become adults every day. That's not the question. The question is, have you contributed to results? It may be work you did yourself or it may be how you served the team and helped them work toward results.

To quickly assess your focus on results, remember to connect your "whats" to your "whys" with the following activity: List your tasks over the past three days. For each task, ask yourself why you do it. You may have to ask why five or six times before you get connected to the organization's results.

Or you might find that you've let yourself become very busy but without doing anything to achieve results. If this is the case, it's time for some serious housecleaning. What are the most critical actions you can take each day that actively help your people and the organization achieve results?

LEAVE A WINNING WELL LEGACY

How will your winning ways survive you? Every day you go about your work; you work with your team to make things, or sell things, or learn things, or work with clients and customers.

If you are especially talented or fortunate, you may make something that endures and changes the world. Maybe. But even if you do make, learn, or sell something amazing, how long will it endure? How long will it have significance?

Long after you finish your reports, spreadsheets, fund-raising, meetings; long after the organization you started or work for has closed, or been sold, or you have left it; long after your daily work is forgotten—what will survive you?

It isn't the "stuff"—the products, the sales, or the decisions. Many times, it's not even the organization. These things are no guarantee of a legacy. It's the people. People are your legacy. The people you helped to win well, who now lead others—others who, in turn, win well themselves.

The final person we want to mention is the late children's TV-show host Fred Rogers. At first glance, the quiet Mr. Rogers and his iconic red sweater may not seem relevant to your management legacy, and yet we can think of few other people who so exemplified Winning Well in their professional life. Rogers understood and articulated the impact you have: "If you could only sense how important you are to the lives of those you meet; how important you can be to the people you may never even dream of. There is something of yourself that you leave at every meeting with another person."

In those remarks upon receiving the Emmy's Lifetime Achievement Award, Rogers encouraged the audience to "take ten seconds to think of the people who have helped you become who you are, those who cared about you and wanted what was best for you in life."

We invite you to reflect as well: Who has helped you become who you are? And now: Who will think of you in the same way?

Long after everything else fades away, it is your influence, your relationships, and how you impact the people around you—these things endure. That's a Winning Well legacy.

YOUR WINNING WELL ACTION PLAN

1. Are you Winning Well? How do you know?

2. What stories will your team share about you?

3. Who will you invite on the Winning Well journey? If you were to share this book with them, would they see you as a role model of the Winning Well behaviors?

4. Make a list of what you want most to be remembered for as a manager. Revisit it from time to time as you work to build your legacy.

Index

9 781400 242382